MYTH

A SYMPOSIUM

MYTH

A SYMPOSIUM

EDITED BY
THOMAS A. SEBEOK

INDIANA UNIVERSITY PRESS
Bloomington and London

CONTENTS

MYTH

A SYMPOSIUM

MYTH, SYMBOLISM, AND TRUTH

BY DAVID BIDNEY

THE problem of myth is one that has concerned Western philosophers from the time of Plato and the Sophists. In Greek thought the problem was to explain the relation of rational, philosophical truth to traditional, religious beliefs, The Sophists of the Greek Enlightenment attempted a reconciliation by interpreting the traditional myths or theogonic tales as allegories revealing naturalistic and moral truths. This allegorical mode of interpretation was criticized by Plato but found continuous favor among the Neo-Platonic and Stoic philosophers of the Hellenistic period who saw in it a method of preserving the authority of tradition as well as the religious prerogatives of the state. The emperor Julian and the philosopher Sallustius regarded myths as divine truths and mysteries hidden from the foolish crowd and apparent only to the wise. By contrast, the Epicurean philosophers since the time of Democritus and Lucretius, the so-called atheists of the ancient world, sought to explain away and get rid of the traditional tales on the ground that they were fabrications which concealed purely naturalistic and historical events at best but were introduced primarily to

3

bolster the authority of the priests and the rulers. Euhemerus in the third century B.C. gave classic expression to this trend of thought and Euhemerism has since become a symbol for all purely historical explanations of myth. In an age which witnessed the deification of actual rulers such as Alexander the Great, it seemed obvious to some philosophers that the traditional myths of gods and heroes concealed no supernatural mysteries but only the prosaic events of actual history at most.

Both the Neo-Platonists and Stoics, as well as the Epicureans, agreed that the myths were not to be taken literally, but the tender-minded conservatives saw in them eternal, allegorical, religious, and philosophical truths, while the tough-minded reformers explained them away as fictions designed to mislead the credulous, superstitious multitude. In the early Christian era, the Christian theologians were glad to avail themselves of the arguments of the Epicureans against the pagan myths while the Stoic and Neo-Platonic philosophers and rulers contended against the Christian claim to exclusive divine revelation. Christian and Hebrew theologians, such as Philo and Saint Augustine, were prepared to interpret the Old Testament narratives allegorically as well as literally but were not willing to acknowledge the same authority to the pagan myths. It is owing largely to Christian influence and intolerance that the pagan religious scriptures have since been regarded in the West as "myths" in the sense of discredited and incredible narratives.

With the advent of the European Renaissance in the fifteenth and sixteenth centuries there was a revival of interest in Greek letters and art. Christian humanism could tolerate an interest in the classic Greek and Roman myths provided they did not compete with the Christian religion. Hence, to the extent that myths could be interpreted as moral allegories or purely poetic or artistic representations of human emotions and aspirations, they were tolerated by the Catholic Church. This tolerance was facilitated by the artistic tradition of the early Church itself which permitted symbolical representation of Christian ideals. The symbol of the Cross and the monogram of Christ, together with such emblems as the Good Shepherd, the Vine, and the Fish, were popularly accepted. During the later Middle Ages Catholic painters were occupied with the representation of subjects of the Old and New Testament history. It was an easy step, therefore, for Renaissance artists to utilize afresh those figures of Greek and Roman mythology which enabled them to express symbolically new secular ideas as, for example, in the work of Titian, Tintoretto, Leonardo, and Michaelangelo. Renaissance art gave symbolic expression to Greek ideals of beauty in the context of Christian culture. Among philosophers, Francis Bacon's attempt in his *The Wisdom of the Ancients* to revive a purely allegorical interpretation of the classic myths as repositories of esoteric philosophical wisdom was not in accord with the culture of the times and received little serious encouragement. The Christian artist could accept Greek ideals of beauty but the Christian philosopher could hardly derive inspiration from their myths.

During the second European Age of Enlightenment in the eighteenth century the typical attitude of the rationalistic philosophers such as Voltaire was to discredit the classic myths either as irrational superstitions or as deliberate fictions foisted upon the multitude by the crafty priests. The point of the attack was to discredit the Hebrew-Christian Scriptures together with the pagan tales as equally untrustworthy. The rationalists were not anti-religious; they sought a religion of reason to replace the religion of faith.

The work of Giovanni Battista Vico stands out as a unique monument of protest against the predominant rationalism of the eighteenth century, which in turn owed so much to the Cartesianism and mathematicism of the seventeenth century. Vico's *New Science* was a seminal work which had substantial influence outside Italy, particularly in Germany, where it was appreciated by men of the stature of Herder and Goethe and influenced the Romantic movement. Vico's method of mythological interpretation may be characterized as "allegorical Euhemerism" since he attempted to reduce the culture heroes of myth to class symbols of society. Vico's method combines an element of allegory together with historic reductionism; myths are taken symbolically as well as literally. He appreciated the ethnological value of myths as containing significant historic records of the cyclical evolution of human thought and social institutions. But the myths were significant not only as ethnological records; they were thought to be originally "true and severe narrations," expressed in poetic language, of actual historical events. In the course of time, Vico held, as later generations failed to understand the true symbolical meaning of these poetic narratives they were altered and finally regarded as incredible.

In the Romantic movement of the late eighteenth century and early nineteenth century, poetic myth became a subject of veneration and was regarded as the mainspring of human culture. In the work of Schelling myth received philosophical justification as an essential element in the philosophy of religion. As Cassirer has observed, Schelling's *Philosophy of Mythology* discards the allegorical interpretation of myth and replaces it by a "tautegorical interpretation" of mythical figures as "autonomous configurations of the human spirit." Myth is said to have its mode of necessity and its own mode of reality. The very intensity with which myth is believed by its adherents excludes any rationalistic theory of pure invention. Myth is not something freely invented by a necessary mode of feeling and belief which appears in the course of history and seizes upon human consciousness. In accordance with Schelling's philosophy of absolute idealism, the mythological process is fundamentally a "theogonic process," that is, a process in which God or the Absolute reveals Himself historically through human consciousness. Man's consciousness had to pass through the mythological stage of polytheism before the true God could be known as such. Mythology is a necessary stage in the self-revelation of the Absolute.

In the Neo-Kantian philosophy of Ernst Cassirer we have the most significant attempt of modern times to construct a philosophy of myth as an integral part of a philosophy of culture. Cassirer's *Philosophy of Symbolic Forms* is an attempt to utilize the positive insights of Schelling while transferring them from a philosophy of absolute idealism to that of the Kantian critical philosophy. Myth is thought of as an autonomous form of the human spirit and hence is not reducible to the play of empirical-psychological forces governing the production of representations. Unlike Schelling, however, Cassirer seeks to explain myth through "the unity of a specific structural form of the spirit," rather than as a theogonic phase of the "absolute process." He is concerned to inquire into the essential character of the mythical function and to contrast this function with that of linguistics, aesthetics, and logic. As he puts it, "A critical phenomenology of the mythical consciousness will start neither from the godhead as an original metaphysical fact nor from mankind as an original empirical fact but will seek to apprehend the subject of the cultural process, the human spirit, solely in its pure actuality and diverse configurations whose immanent forms it will strive to ascertain."[1] Myth creates a world of its own in accordance with a spiritual principle, a world which discloses an immanent rule, a characteristic necessity. The objectivity of myth consists in its being a concrete and necessary mode of spiritual formation, "a typical mode of formation in which consciousness disengages itself from and confronts the mere receptivity of the sensory impression."

Cassirer observes that for Schelling all mythology was essentially the theory and history of the gods. Schelling's philosophy of myth, like the ethnological theories of Andrew Lang, Wilhelm Schmidt, and Wilhelm Koppers, presupposes a primary original monotheism followed by a mythological polytheism. Cassirer, however, is inclined to accept the views of Preuss, Vierkandt, and Marett, that primitive religion began with an entirely undifferentiated intuition of a magical, extraordinary power inherent in things. The primitive, mythopoeic mind, he maintains, is to be studied empirically and functionally without any preconceived metaphysical notions.

According to Cassirer, mythical thinking is a unitary form of consciousness with its specific and characteristic features. There is no unity of object in myth but only a unity of function expressed in a unique mode of experience. Hence he is opposed to all forms of "nature mythology" which would explain the origin of myth by reference to some particular class of natural objects, such as astral mythology. Unity of explanation is to be sought only in unity of function, in unity of cultural sphere and structured form.

Ultimately the unity of myth is to be sought not in a genetic and causal explanation but in a teleological sense as a direction followed by consciousness in constructing spiritual real-

ity. It is Cassirer's self-imposed task to inquire into the
nature of that formal unity through which the infinitely mul-
tiform world of myth constitutes a characteristic spiritual
whole. Myth is an autonomous cultural form and must not be
"explained" by reduction to some other symbolic form, such
as language. Max Müller's attempt to explain the origin of
myth in linguistic ambivalence as a kind of "disease of language" is a case in point. Not unity of origin, whether in
language or natural object, but unity of structure and function, as revealed in the end or final product, is the true objective. Myth is not a reflection of an objective reality independent of it, but is rather the product of true creative,
spiritual actions, an independent image world of the spirit as
well as an active force of expression. Myth is the first expression of a spiritual process of liberation which is effected in
the progress from the magical-mythical world view to the
truly religious view. Myth is the first step in "the dialectic
of bondage and liberation which the human spirit experiences
with its own self-made image worlds."

In the beginning of human culture myth is not yet sharply
differentiated from other cultural forms. Thus language, like
myth, preserves a complete equivalence of world and thing
and only gradually acquires its own spiritual form and sig-
nificatory function. Similarly in art there is at first no sharp
differentiation between the real and the ideal. Art also is
embedded at first in magical representations, and the image
has no purely aesthetic significance. Thus, although myth,
language, and art interpenetrated one another originally in
primitive culture, there is a progressive development to the
point where the human spirit becomes conscious of the diver-
sity and relative autonomy of its self-created symbols. Science is distinguished from other forms of cultural life in that
through science the human mind knows its symbols as symbols distinct from sense impressions. But this spiritual freedom of self-consciousness is the result of a long process of
critical endeavor.

According to Cassirer's Neo-Kantian approach, we must
understand the mythical symbol, not as a representation con-
cealing some mystery or hidden truth, but as a self-contained
form of interpretation of reality. In myth there is no distinc-

tion between the real and the ideal; the image is the thing and hence mythical thinking lacks the category of the ideal. This is true in all stages of mythical thinking and is expressed most clearly in mythical action. In all mythical action the subject of the rite is transformed into a god or demon whom he represents. Hence Cassirer is prepared to admit with Robertson-Smith that rites precede myth and that the narrative of myth is a mediate interpretation of the immediately given rite. This explains why rites are taken so seriously in primitive religion and why it is constantly believed that the continuance of human life and the very survival of the world depend on the correct performance of rites. Nature is thought to yield nothing without ceremonies. Thus in the dance as well as in fertility rites the human actor does not regard himself as engaging in mere imitative representation but as becoming identified momentarily with the person of the mythical drama and exercising his powers. Similarly, word and name do not merely designate and signify objects; they are the essence of the thing and contain its magical powers. In like manner, the image of a thing is endowed with its active force and what happens to the image happens also to the object—a basic assumption of much of primitive magic. Thus in primitive language, art, and magic, mythical thinking uses symbolic representations but without differentiating the symbols from their objects.

This would seem to imply that the Neo-Kantian theory of the constitutive character of symbolism is in accord with the practice of primitive culture and would be valid for us *if* we adhered to primitive rites and mythical beliefs. Cassirer himself arrived at the "astonishing conclusion" that David Hume, in attempting to analyze the causal judgment of science, rather revealed a source of all mythical explanation of the world. One feels tempted to say that Cassirer, in attempting to analyze the constructive functions of cultural symbols in constituting objective reality, succeeded only in revealing an implicit assumption of all mythological thought but *not* of critical philosophical and scientific thought, as he thought he had done.

According to Cassirer, myth has a truth of its own distinct from that of other cultural forms since the mythical mind is creative and gives expression to its own form of objective reality. That is why he insists that myth is to be interpreted literally and is opposed to allegorical interpretation on the ground that the latter reduces myth to some other mode of cultural truth such as philosophy, religion, or history, and does not account for the unique and irreducible element in mythical expression.

We are then faced with the problem: what is this ideal, distinctive function of myth? What is myth apart from its expression in primitive word-magic, ritual-magic, and image-magic? If myth as narrative is merely the mediate interpretation of the immediately given rite, in what sense is myth an autonomous expression with a truth of its own? Since all mythical thinking is said to confuse the ideal and the real, the symbol and its object, in what sense then does myth convey a truth of its own through its autonomous symbolic forms?

Cassirer has demonstrated how language gradually frees itself from the mythological context, and how the notion of language as a distinct symbolic form emerges. There is crisis or breaking point in the development of language at which the symbolic, semantic function of language becomes clearly differentiated from its objects. Similarly, religion breaks away from its mythical foundations and assumes its own form. Religious dogma is said to be the form assumed by pure religious meaning when men seek to express this meaning in terms of objective representations. In religious mysticism both the mythical and the dogmatic elements of faith are rejected and the incarnation of God is understood as a process which operates continuously in human consciousness. In the religious consciousness, however, the conflict between the pure meaning and the mythical image is never really resolved. Only in the sphere of art, Cassirer maintains, does the opposition between image and meaning become resolved, for only in the aesthetic consciousness is the image recognized as such.[2] The aesthetic consciousness which gives itself over to pure contemplation finally achieves a pure spiritualization of symbolic expression and a maximum of freedom.

One is compelled to conclude reluctantly that in his *Philosophy of Symbolic Forms* Cassirer has not demonstrated his thesis that myth is an autonomous form of symbolism. For him, as for the ethnologists and philosophers whom he criticized, myth is a stage in the development of culture. Far from being an autonomous and integral segment of universal human culture, it is rather a mode of thought based on the confusion of the symbolic ideal and the existential real which manifests itself historically at a given stage of cultural evolution. In the progressive development of human conciousness the symbolic functions of language, art, religion, and science are gradually differentiated from the mythological-magical complex, though traces of their mythic origin remain. At most it may be said that for Cassirer myth is a necessary stage in the creative expression and self-liberation of the human spirit. But since Cassirer acknowledges no metaphysical Absolute as does Schelling, the mythic symbols may not be said to express an implicit religious truth, but only the delusions of the primitive human consciousness as it struggles to interpret the world of experience and reality. Ironically, it may be said that Cassirer's Neo-Kantian vision of a synthesis of symbolic forms each of which is constitutive of objective reality is in agreement with the implicit assumptions of mythological thought, but fails to account for the critical, transcultural validity and objectivity of philosophical and scientific thought which he himself sought to establish.

In his later works, notably in the *Essay on Man* and his posthumous *The Myth of the State,* Cassirer returned to the problem of myth, apparently feeling dissatisfied with his treatment in the earlier work. In his *Essay* he stated that in myth one observes not objective but "physiognomic characters."[3] The world of myth is said to be a dramatic world, a world of conflicting powers, and mythical perception is impregnated with these emotional qualities. While all efforts of scientific thought are directed towards eliminating the subjective, physiognomic perception of nature, the "anthropological value" of the data of physiognomic experience remains unchanged. "Science delimits their objectivity, but it cannot completely destroy their reality." The mythic perception is just as real as the scientific since every feature of our human experience has a claim to reality. Thus myth may be said to contribute a truth of its own as a distinct, qualitative way of envisaging reality through its own symbolic forms and categories.

It is important to note here that myth has no explanatory value as an interpretation of nature. The nature myths with their poetic language and physiognomic characterizations comprise a record of uncritical human experience and constitute "a step on our way to reality." The "truth" of myth is a purely subjective, psychological truth and expresses how reality appears in terms of our human feeling-qualities. In this sense myth is real, just as every psychological experience is real to the subject.

On this evaluation, the "truth" of myth is then purely subjective and differs in no significant way from the purely subjective "truth" of a delusion. This is hardly an argument for the autonomy of myth as a distinct symbolic form with an objective validity comparable to that of science. To argue for the reality of mythical experience in the minds of certain believers is not to establish its autonomy as a distinct symbolic form. The significant question is whether myth may be said to have an objective truth and value of its own, and Cassirer's argument, so far, suggests that it has none. If it be true that "in the new light of science mythical perception has to fade away,"[4] and that myths have no cosmological value, then their so-called "anthropological value" is of no significance other than as a record of precritical human experience.

Far from denying that myths have no objective explanatory value, Cassirer makes a special point of admitting it. The unity of myth is said to consist in a unity of function rather than of object, but this function is not that of explanation. In *The Myth of the State* he develops the thesis that myths are primarily emotional in origin, and that their function is essentially practical and social, namely, to promote a feeling of unity or harmony between the members of a society as well as a sense of harmony with the whole of nature or life. This theory of the pragmatic function of myth is one which Cassirer admittedly derived in large measure from Malinowski, to whom he often refers.

Here we must differentiate between Cassirer's views as to the psychological motivation of the mythopoeic mind and his evaluation of the sociological function of myth. The psychological motivation of myth-making explains the origin of this activity as a direct expression of human feeling rather than of intellectual thought. "The realm substratum of myth is not a substratum of thought but of feeling."[5] Religion and myth are said to give us a "unity of feeling," whereas art provides a unity of intuition, and science comprises a unity of thought.[6] On this psychological premise, myth provides a rationalization and validation of human emotions rather than an objective explanation of nature. In this respect Cassirer's position is anti-intellectual since it reduces the function of thought in primitive culture to a secondary position and gives the primacy to feeling and action. Man acts first and rationalizes his conduct later. This is the psychological basis for Cassirer's acceptance of the historical priority of ritual to myth.

The notion of a "unity of feeling" turns out to be rather complex. First, it refers to the fact that myth and religion have a common origin in human feeling considered as a separate mental faculty. Second, "unity of feeling" has an ontological import and refers to "the solidarity of life." This renders intelligible the outstanding feature of the mythical world, "the law of metamorphosis"[7] in virtue of which everything may be turned into everything. Hence primitive man's view of nature is said to be neither theoretical nor practical, but sentimental and "sympathetic." Primitive man has a deep immediate feeling of the fundamental solidarity of life that underlies the multiplicity of its forms. "To mythical and religious feeling nature becomes one great society, the society of life."[8] When, therefore, Cassirer speaks of the sociological function of myth he finds it easy to make the transition from this metaphysical principle of cosmic sympathy to the notion of the solidarity of human society. With Durkheim and Malinowski he maintains that the pragmatic function of myth is to promote social solidarity as well as solidarity with nature as a whole in time of social crises. Mythical thought is especially concerned to deny and negate the fact of death and to affirm the unbroken unity and continuity of life.[9]

I would differentiate, therefore, the *unity of feeling* considered as a mental faculty from the *feeling of unity* which is a metabiological assumption of the indestructible unity of life. One may maintain the theory that mythical thought implicitly presupposes the latter metaphysical assumption without affirming the former psychological thesis that myth originates in the faculty of feeling rather than of thought. Cassirer, however, does not make this distinction clear and speaks as if unity of feeling and feeling of unity were identical.

Cassirer makes the point in his *Myth of the State* that he does not wish to maintain the thesis that myth originates solely in emotion. "Myth," he states, "cannot be described as bare emotion because it is the *expression* of emotion. The expression of a feeling is not the feeling itself—it is emotion turned into image."[10] Mythical symbolism leads to an objectification of feelings; myth objectifies and organizes human hopes and fears and metamorphosizes them into persistent and durable works. Myth is then a symbolic expression of emotion and instinct with an objective character of its own and it is this symbolic expression which differentiates the work of myth from animal reactions.

On the other hand, man's metabiological impulse to identify himself with, and participate in, the life of nature as a whole leads him to express himself directly in symbolic rites of a religious-magical character in order to ensure his survival and well-being. In myth these ritual acts are "explained" and validated. Thus myth is a unique form of symbolism which supervenes upon the symbolism of ritual in order to validate and perpetuate it. It is not at all clear from Cassirer's account why myth may not be a direct symbolic expression of human emotion without prior reference to ritual. In any event, myth is not a conscious creation or invention of individuals but is rather a product of man's spontaneous expression of emotion and feeling of unity with nature as a whole. Myth differs from art precisely in the fact that the mythical imagination and intuition imply a *belief* in the reality of its object.[11] The mythopoeic mind does not regard myth merely as a symbolic expression or representation of some independent reality; the mythic symbols are identical with the reality.[12] Hence mythical reality is accepted as given and is not subjected to critical evaluation.

Here I would distinguish further two distinct points which

are implicit in Cassirer's argument: first, myth is said to be *based on belief* in the reality of its objects and the truth of its intuitions of the unity of nature and solidarity of life; second, myth is said to have the pragmatic function of *promoting belief* in the solidarity of life and society and in overcoming the fear of death. According to the first argument, ritual acts already presuppose an intuition of cosmic unity of life and a feeling of identity of man with nature. On the other hand, if the function of myth is to promote belief in the solidarity of life then this mythic belief is independent of ritual and the latter becomes intelligible only as a function or consequent of myth. There is, it seems to me, a real issue here which Cassirer did not resolve. He tended to agree with Malinowski in stressing the social and pragmatic function of myth in the crises of life and with Robertson-Smith in granting the priority of ritual to myth. He did not realize that his pragmatic, utilitarian approach to myth failed to account for the *fact of belief* which is presupposed in myth but which the myth itself does not produce. Malinowski's pragmatic theory implies the notion of myth as a kind of unconscious, or conscious, fiction which supervenes upon institutional rites—a thesis which Cassirer himself rejects as incompatible with his evolutionary approach to symbolic forms.[13]

To my way of thinking, the central and inescapable issue is the relevance of the question of truth to mythic belief. If myth be conceived as an intrinsically subjective mode of experience, then it may be said to have a purely psychological and ethnological value as a record and expression of uncritical, "physiognomic" emotional experience. The "truth" of myth would then lie in its factual and historical subjectivity. But if the mythic and religious intuition of the solidarity and continuity of cosmic life be accepted as true in the sense of being in accord with a non-mythic reality, then myth may be interpreted allegorically. Since Cassirer does not acknowledge any reality other than symbolic reality, the idea of a non-symbolic reality as a referent for myth is precluded. His only alternative is to suggest, following Durkheim, that myth has a sociological or anthropological value. Not nature but society is the model of myth.[14] Myth refers to a social reality, to the rites and institutions of society, and hence the truth of myth consists in its symbolic representation of social rites.[15] In this way Cassirer thought to avoid an allegorical interpretation of myth while providing an objective social referent for mythic symbolism.

Cassirer saw no contradiction in following simultaneously both a metaphysical and a sociological approach.[16] According to his metaphysical approach, myth is based on a primitive intuition of the cosmic solidarity of life and hence he affirms that myth is potential religion. In so far as he follows the sociological approach of Durkheim and Malinowski myth is said to rationalize and validate ritual and metamorphose human hopes and fears, especially the fear of death.

The truth of myth is then a function of the interpretation of myth. If one accepts the truth of the original intuition of the solidarity of life and the dramatic character of its underlying forces then myth symbolizes allegorically a fundamental metaphysical and religious truth. For the sociological approach, however, the truth of myth consists in its symbolic expression of ritual and has no cosmic reference. Cassirer, it appears, was not prepared to acknowledge the rational validity of the primitive intuition of the organic and cosmic solidarity of all life. His only alternatives were to accept either a purely subjective truth of the reality of mythic experience, or else an objective sociological truth which reduced myth to the secondary role of symbolizing ritual. In either case, it is difficult to see how he could defend his original thesis that myth is an autonomous form of symbolism comparable to language, art, and science.

Among American philosophers, W. M. Urban follows most closely the Neo-Kantian views of Cassirer on the positive value of mythic symbolism. In his *Language and Reality* Urban agrees that myth is a unique way of apprehending the world and has its own categories and presuppositions. Urban accepts the mythical origin of the primary religious symbols and hence maintains that myth provides the material of religious symbolism. Nevertheless, myth and religion are not identical. "Neither the form nor the spirit of the two is the same."[17] While the religious consciousness expresses its insights in the language of myth, this does not mean literal acceptance of, and belief in, myths. Myths are interpreted "symbolically" for their ideal meaning. In religion mythical language is used to symbolize a non-mythical reality. Myth is said to be "indispensable" to religion for the reason that it is impossible to separate the language of myth from that of religion. From an epistemological point of view myth is said to be indispensable because it is a primary and unique way of apprehending reality, which gives expression to qualities and values which elude the symbolism of science.[18] Finally, myth employs a dramatic language and only dramatic language is ultimately intelligible. Myth is, therefore, to be taken seriously, but it may not be taken literally.

It should be noted that while Urban agrees with Cassirer in his positive acceptance of myth, he does so for different reasons. According to Urban, all symbolism has a dual character and embraces the real and the unreal, truth and fiction.[19] Hence the symbol is not identical with objective reality, even though it is only through symbolic forms that the mind comprehends and communicates its knowledge of reality. Mythical symbols are, therefore, said to symbolize a non-mythical, non-symbolic reality. For Cassirer, on the other hand, the symbol is constitutive of reality; there is no objective reality or thing-in-itself other than symbolic reality. Hence, if myth is to be taken seriously, it must be taken literally as well.

Cassirer's theory of the function of human emotion in originating myth and religion is reminiscent in many essentials of Bergson's *The Two Sources of Morality and Religion* to which he refers. According to Bergson, there are two sources of morality and religion, both of which are biological in the sense of being rooted in the nature of man. First, there is the infra-rational social impulse, which man shares in part with animals, to seek solidarity with his group as well as with nature which is the source of life. Second, there is the supra-rational intuition, characteristic of man alone, whereby he comprehends the absolute or divine source of his being. The infra-rational impulse is the source of the closed, static society and social morality; it manifests itself culturally in the presence of society and conformity to social customs. The supra-rational intuition is the source of the open, progressive society, of a human morality and heroic, individual aspiration. There is a difference in kind, and not merely in degree, between these two types of morality and religion.

The role of the intellect is conceived as secondary to emotion and intuition; intellect mediates between the unconscious impulses of the infra-rational and the mystic intuitions of the supra-rational. According to Bergson, "Man, fresh from the hands of nature, was a being both intelligent and social, his sociability being devised to find its scope in small communities, his intelligence being designed to further individual and group life."[20] The primary function of intelligence is to find means of promoting social solidarity and regulating it by means of rules and principles. Reason itself is not the source of moral obligation as the Kantian idealists maintain; moral obligation is rooted in emotion and impulse, in the biological necessities of life.

But rational intelligence tends in time to defeat this "intention" of nature by alienating the individual from his society and from nature. The function or utility of the myth-making imagination, and of religion which is its product, is to counteract this tendency of the intelligence to break up the cohesion of society while promoting individual freedom and initiative. "Religion," according to Bergson, "is a defensive reaction of nature against the dissolvent power of intelligence."[21] In particular, religion is a defense reaction against the intellectual notion of the inevitability of death. Religion is not motivated by fear, but is a positive reaction against the fears induced by the intellect.

Myth in general (including religion) is a joint product of instinct and intelligence introduced to counteract the destructive and devisive activities of intelligence and to promote belief in the solidarity of life. The myths and superstitions of man have a positive biological function in promoting life and in counteracting the excesses of intelligence which threaten the individual and his society. Hence we are confronted with the apparent paradox "that an essentially intelligent being is naturally superstitious, and that intelligent creatures are the only superstitious beings."[22]

Bergson's position on myth is then characterized by a positive as well as negative attitude. Like the rationalists he tends to identify myth with unconscious fiction and superstition, but at the same time he recognizes the pragmatic, biological value of myth in its religious form in counteracting the excesses of intelligence and in promoting a positive faith in the continuity of life. The final objectives and consequences of religious myth are sound and are in accord with the "intentions" of nature and in this sense myth may be said to conceal the wisdom of nature. But myth is not the only social instrument of nature in the service of man. Through supra-rational intuition and divine revelation there is revealed an absolute truth and a transcendental morality which inspires man to free himself from his mythical superstitions and the pressures of static, closed society. A true, dynamic morality and religion do not require the myth-making functions characteristic of primitive cultures.

Finally, according to the ethnological work of the French ethnologist Maurice Leenhardt, as interpreted recently by Eric Dardel in his essay on "The Mythic,"[23] myth is to be understood as a "reaction to reality." For Dardel, myth is infra-rational but coexists with reason and complements it. Myth is said to be "neither 'true' nor 'false'; it is beyond our logic's horizon, in that 'pang' which comes upon man in the midst of things. In the myth and by means of the mythic image, there is an externalisation of the inner stirring, the emotion of man as he meets the world, his receptivity to impulses coming from 'outside,' the communality of substance which welds him to the totality of beings."[24]

Man's interpretation of the world is said to have evolved through three stages: a mythic stage, an epic stage, and a historical stage. The mythic stage changes into the epic stage when man bases his conduct on some notion of "the model man," or the cult of the hero. The historic stage emerges when man ceases to look to the exemplary past and sets up for himself rational objectives and means for their attainment.

Following Lévy-Bruhl, Cassirer, and Bergson, Dardel stresses the point that myth is closely bound up with emotion and "renounces reflection." Myth involves strong emotional attachments and beliefs in "verities" which are declared to be true. As Dardel puts it, "Every period declares 'its' truth in this way and is warmly attached to it. Our 'truth' of the moment is often only a myth that does not know it is one, and, as M. Jourdain put it, we make myths every day without knowing it."[25] The myth-making function is a universal and fundamental phenomenon of whose emotional motivation the mind is largely unconscious.

Dardel is also in basic agreement with Bergson and Cassirer that myth is the common source of morality and religion. The fundamental religious myth, he maintains, is not the story of the gods, but the totemic myth from which the myth of the gods evolves. In this respect his position conforms to that of Durkheim.

With the advent of rationality or the *Logos,* myth loses ground and is "driven back into the shadows." Dardel agrees with Bergson that the victory of *Logos* is not necessarily beneficial to man. The ground lost by myth is not always won by reason and freedom. Unlike Bergson, however, Dardel has no alternative to myth other than reason. He is, therefore, inclined to fall back on Jung's theory that myth is always a typical story, an archaic type with exemplary value. Hence, far from disparaging and distrusting myth, he counsels that "it is better above all to lend an ear to this mythic, underlying our own reason and knowing, which the work of Jung and his school have brought to light as one of the great realities of our mental life."[26] Myth, though based on instinct and emotion, contains an unconscious wisdom; it is not something to be superseded by science, even though it may assume the face of science and the diction of reason. Our basic social faiths, like those of primitive man, are grounded in myth. This explains "the impassioned tonality which makes certain 'verities' vibrate inside us, which ought to remain serene and indifferent to contradiction. The myth is what we never see in ourselves, the secret spring of our vision of the world, of our devotion, of our dearest notions."[27]

In sum, myth, is beyond truth and falsity. The "truth" of myth is a function of its pragmatic and dramatic effectiveness in moving men to act in accordance with typical, emotionally charged ideals. The effectiveness of myth depends in large measure upon ignorance or unconsciousness of its actual motivation. That is why myth tends to recede before the advance of reason and self-conscious reflection. But myth has a perennial function to perform in providing a basis for social faith and action. Our myths are rooted in the collective unconscious, and we are most in their power when we are unconscious of their origin.

The history of mythological theory demonstrates that there have been two basic approaches to the interpretation of myth, the literal and the symbolic. On the whole, ethnologists have tended to interpret myth literally as an expression of primitive thought but have differed in their evaluation of myth. Evolutionary, positivistic ethnologists, such as Tylor, have regarded myth negatively as a mode of explanatory thought destined to be superseded by scientific thought. Functionalistic ethnologists, such as Malinowski, have evaluated myth in terms of its pragmatic function in resolving critical problems which affect the welfare and destiny of the individaul and his society. Myths are then said to validate institutions and rites. They are rationalizations introduced to justify established social facts. Pragmatic philosophers and sociologists, such as Sorel and Pareto, have recognized cynically the fictional character of myth but have nevertheless justified its use as an instrument of policy and social control. Bergson, we have seen, saw in myth an expression of the cunning of nature and intelligence designed to counteract the excesses of intelligence in alienating man from society and nature. So understood, myth has a limited biological value which may be superseded in so far as man is motivated to act by his suprarational intuitions and aspirations.

On the other hand, idealistic philosophers and theologians have, from ancient to modern times, interpreted myth allegorically as symbolizing some transcendental, timeless truth but have differed among themselves as to the nature of the object and truth so symbolized. In contemporary thought, myth has been evaluated positively owing in large measure to the influence of psychoanalytical theory, especially that of Jung. In philosophy and religion, Neo-Kantian philosophers, such as Cassirer and Urban, and theologians of the stature

of Nicolas Berdyaev and Richard Neibuhr, have advocated
a positive evaluation of myth. In the sphere of literary criticism, scholars such as Northrop Frye, Maud Bodkin, and
most recently Philip Wheelwright, have taken myth seriously
as symbolizing universal archetypes and "primordial images"
emerging from the collective unconscious. The positive value
of myth is affirmed by those who are skeptical of the power
of reason to comprehend reality, or the revelations of intuition, as well as by those who accept the position of linguistic
and symbolic relativism and adhere to the theory that symbols have no truth-value but only a moral, poetic value as
regulative ideals.

My own thesis is that a scientific study of myth should be
concerned with the comparative and historical analysis of
myth and that myth should be interpreted literally. Myth
has a positive value for the ethnologist and folklorist as a
record of man's culture history and as a means of establish-
ing universal patterns of thought. Myth, like great art and
dramatic literature, may have profound symbolic or allegorical value for us of the present, not because myth necessarily
and intrinsically has such latent, esoteric wisdom, but because the plot or theme suggests to us universal patterns of
motivation and conduct. It must not be assumed, however,
that the subjective, symbolic value of a myth for us and the
actual historical beliefs of its originators are identical.

Further, as indicated in *Theoretical Anthropology,* I
should maintain that myth is a universal cultural phenomenon originating in a plurality of motives and involving all
mental faculties. As products of the creative intelligence of
man myths may refer to any class of objects whatsoever, and
hence I regard all attempts to reduce myth to some monistic
class of objects as essentially misleading. I am inclined also
to question seriously the notion of a mythopoeic mind, or a
special faculty or form of mythic symbolism as advocated
by Cassirer and Urban. Myth originates wherever thought
and imagination are employed uncritically or deliberately
used to promote social delusion. All mental functions may
contribute to the formation of myth, and there is historically
an essential similarity in the psychological functions involved
in its emergence and diffusion. All that changes is the type

of myth which prevails at different times and in different cultures. In prescientific cultures animistic myths and magical rites tend to prevail. In our secular, scientific cultures we have naturalistic social myths reflecting ethnocentrism and deliberate falsification in the interests of propaganda. The social and political myths of our time, the effective social faith which guides national policy, are often the product of the divorce of scientific thought from the social values and beliefs which motivate our conduct. The tragic element in all this is the fact that this separation of science and values has been brought about in no small measure by a deliberate restriction of the function of science and scientific method to non-cultural data.

My conclusion is that while in times of crisis the "noble fiction" may have its immediate, pragmatic utility in promoting social faith and solidarity, faith in reason and in the ability of democratic man to govern himself rationally requires a minimum of reliance upon myth. To my mind, contemporary philosophers and theologians, as well as students of literature in general, who speak of the "indispensable myth" in the name of philosophy and religion, and anthropologists and sociologists who cynically approve of myth because of its pragmatic social function, are undermining faith in their own disciplines and are contributing unwittingly to the very degradation of man and his culture which they otherwise seriously deplore. Myth must be taken seriously as a cultural force but it must be taken seriously precisely in order that it may be gradually superseded in the interests of the advancement of truth and the growth of human intelligence. Normative, critical, and scientific thought provides the only self-correcting means of combating the diffusion of myth, but it may do so only on condition that we retain a firm and uncompromising faith in the integrity of reason and in the transcultural validity of the scientific enterprise.

NOTES

1. Ernst Cassirer, *The Philosophy of Symbolic Forms,* II (New Haven, 1955), 13.

2. Cassirer, *The Philosophy of Symbolic Forms,* II, 261.

3. Ernst Cassirer, *Essay on Man* (New Haven, 1944), p. 76.

4. Cassirer, *Essay on Man,* p. 77.

5. Cassirer, *Essay on Man,* p. 81.

6. Ernst Cassirer, *Myth of the State* (New Haven, 1946), p. 37.

7. Cassirer, *Essay on Man,* p. 81.

8. Cassirer, *Essay on Man,* p. 83.

9. Cassirer, *Essay on Man,* p. 84.

10. Cassirer, *Myth of the State,* p. 43.

11. Cassirer, *Essay on Man,* p. 75.

12. Cassirer, *Myth of the State,* p. 47.

13. Cassirer, *Essay on Man,* p. 74.

14. Cassirer, *Essay on Man,* p. 79.

15. Cassirer, *Myth of the State,* p. 28.

16. David Bidney, *Theoretical Anthropology* (New York, 1953), p. 317.

17. W. M. Urban, *Language and Reality* (London, 1939), p. 592.

18. Urban, *Language and Reality,* p. 593.

19. Urban, *Language and Reality,* p. 420.

20. Bergson, *The Two Sources of Morality and Religion,* Doubleday Anchor Books ed. (New York, 1954), p. 57.

21. Bergson, *The Two Sources of Morality,* p. 122.

22. Bergson, *The Two Sources of Morality,* p. 109.

23. Eric Dardel, "The Mythic," *Diogenes,* No. 7 (Summer, 1954), pp. 33-51.

24. Dardel, "The Mythic," p. 36.

25. Dardel, "The Mythic," p. 37.

26. Dardel, "The Mythic," p. 42.

27. Dardel, "The Mythic," p. 50.

THE ECLIPSE OF
SOLAR MYTHOLOGY

BY RICHARD M. DORSON

WE smile condescendingly today at the solar mythologists. So restrained a scholar as Stith Thompson refers to the extinct school as "absurd," "fantastic," "ridiculous," even dangerous to the sanity of the modern reader.[1] Max Müller and his disciples are chided for not recognizing the inanity of their own theories, and Andrew Lang is lauded for piercing them with ridicule.

Max Müller's sun has indeed set. But was the leading Sanscrit scholar of his day a fool? And why did Lang have to spend a quarter of a century in demolishing ideas so patently absurd? The famous *Chips* now sell at the old-book stalls for ten cents a volume, but they once graced the parlor tables of thoughtful Victorians, and in at least one instance distracted a groom on his honeymoon.[2] Viewed as part of the intellectual growth of the nineteenth century, solar mythology assumes a more honorable aspect.[3] Its devotees contributed a yeasty ferment to the newly baptized field of folklore, and drew the attention of a host of scholars and readers to traditional narratives. Thompson neglects to comment on the intensity and drama of this fray, nor does he indicate that it was a two-way battle, lethal for both combatants. For Müller gave as good as he received, and riddled Lang's own cherished concept of "savage" survivals. Before the smoke had cleared, this acrid debate over the origins of myths had greatly broadened the base of folklore scholarship.

Solar mythology primarily deserves the attention of folklore students for the role it played in the history of our subject. In England, where the leading action took place, the comparative mythologists asserted and defended their position throughout the second half of the nineteenth century. As Lang himself conceded, without their provocation he and his fellow-folklorists might never have stirred into existence. One wonders indeed what Lang could have written on folklore without the enticing target of Müller, whose name re-echoes on Lang's pages; if Müller were a dying god, apparently he enjoyed successive rebirths, for the Scot kept slaying him through numerous publications. To unravel this intricate literature of controversy, bursting into many books, dipping frequently into periodical essays and reviews, and spreading across the continent, would require another book. This paper will confine itself to England, and to the two principal protagonists, with some consideration of Müller's chief allies, George W. Cox and Robert Brown, and of two American supporters, Daniel G. Brinton and John Fiske.

The historian of any field of learning would be proud to relate the encounter of two such brilliant luminaries as Andrew Lang and the Right Honorable Friedrich Max Müller. Between them they furnished English gentlemen with a well-stocked library. Coming to England from his native Germany as a youth of twenty-six, eager to translate the Sacred Books of India, Max Müller settled in Oxford and never left. He won a vast audience with limpid essays on such forbidding subjects as the science of language and the religion of India, and became so famous that when he considered leaving Oxford University in 1875 at the invitation of European governments, a special decree at Convocation and a prayerful eulogy from the Dean of Christ Church broke precedent to retain him free from all teaching duties.[4] When Müller died in 1900, Queen Victoria sent his widow a personal telegram of sympathy, and royalty around the world added their condolences.

Andrew Lang, who would survive his adversary twelve years, wrote a gracious letter to Mrs. Max Müller, and spoke of her husband's "good humour and kindness perhaps unexampled in the controversies of the learned and half-learned."[5] Classical "performer," essayist, historian, poet, critic, anthropologist, sports writer, Lang ranged over so many fields of letters and learning that today a whole battery of specialists deliver lectures at St. Andrews on his contributions to their chosen fields.[6] His fecundity and wit were the despair of his contemporaries, who writhed from his thrusts in the evening papers, the weekly and monthly reviews, and the endless books he wrote, edited and prefaced.[7]

In 1856 Max Müller published a long essay on "Comparative Mythology" which reoriented all previous thinking on the origin of myths. The treatise astonished and delighted philologists, classicists, and literary scholars; John Fiske recalls the excitement that swept him on first reading the "noble essay," and Cox and Lang equally pay it tribute.[8] Only ten years earlier William Thoms had devised the term "folk-lore" to embrace the study of popular antiquities, and had begun comparative annotations of beliefs and tales in *Notes and Queries*. Only five years before had the first book appeared which used "Folklore" in its title.[9] The study of mythology remained in a separate, sterile compartment; even Thomas Keightley, who wrote on both fairy legends and Greek myths, produced only a conventional manual of classical mythology interpreting the Homeric gods and heroes as pretty allegories.[10] Müller now offered a key to the understanding of Aryan traditions, whether myths of the gods, legends of heroes, or tales of the people, through the science of comparative philology and the new revelation of Vedic Sanscrit.

From the appearance of this essay to the last years of his life Müller expanded and championed his method. The *Lectures on the Science of Language, Second Series* (1864) included five chapters relating to solar mythology. Three years later Müller brought together in the second volume of his *Chips from a German Workshop* his occasional "Essays on Mythology, Traditions, and Customs" dating from (and including) his epochal monograph. This volume particularly intrigues the intellectual historian by recording Müller's reactions, in the form of review-essays, to classical folklore works emerging in the 1860's: the tale-collections of Callaway, Dasent, and Campbell, and the seminal researches of Tylor. A lecture "On the Philosophy of Mythology" formed part of the *Introduction to the Science of Religion* (1873).[11] In his *Lectures on the Origin and Growth of Religion, as illustrated by the religions of India* (1878), Müller turned critic, and to the question "Is Fetishism a Primitive Form of Religion?" replied with a strong negative; at the same time he discussed the problem of securing reliable evidence from savages on their beliefs. Here Müller strikes at the anthropological evolutionists. The chapters on "The Lessons of the Veda" and "Vedic Deities" in *India: What Can It Teach Us* (1882) tentatively apply the solar theory to savages.

He considerably extended his critique of rival methods in analyzing the three schools of mythology contending in England. In *Physical Religion* (1891), Müller devoted particular attention to Agni, the Vedic god of fire, and demonstrated his religious and mythological components in two chapters, "The Mythological Development of Agni" and "Religion, Myth, and Custom." Again in *Anthropological Religion* (1892), the four-time Gifford lecturer touched on such favorite themes as the unreliability of anthropological evidence, and the contradictory reports about savage ideas and ways. Because mythology formed a vital link in his chain of being, along with thought, language, and religion, Müller rarely omitted the solar theory from his general discussions of cultural and religious origins. In these books Müller never mentioned Lang by name, although he referred continually to "ethno-psychological" mythologists who studied the tales of savages without learning their languages. Lang remarked on this omission in his review of a new edition of the *Chips* (1894), a review which finally drew blood and led Müller to produce two thick volumes on *Contributions to the Science of Mythology* (1897).[12] Here he massed the arguments of his lifelong researches for a personal clash with Lang, repeated everything he had previously written, and repeated his repetitions throughout the twin volumes.

Lang was equally voluminous and repetitious. He tells us that, with other undergraduates at Oxford in the 1860's, he read Müller's writings on mythology, without conviction; after graduating in 1868, his reading in the myths of savage races hardened his distrust of Müller into a contrary hypothesis.[13] The first fruits of this thinking appeared in a ground-breaking article, "Mythology and Fairy Tales," published in the *Fortnightly Review* in 1872. Lang continued to snipe away in the magazines at Müller's solar interpretations[14] until the year 1884, when he unloosed a formidable barrage of more permanent criticism. He gathered together his essays illustrating the anthropological approach and undermining the philological method, in *Custom and Myth,* a popular work which enjoyed frequent reprintings. A major article on "Mythology" in the ninth edition of the *Encyclopaedia Britannica,* subsequently translated into French in book form,[15] closely examined and dissected Müller's theory. A detailed introduction to Margaret Hunt's translation of Grimm's *Household Tales* paid special attention to the hypotheses of Müller's leading disciple, George W. Cox. When Müller wrote three articles in the *Nineteenth Century* in 1885 confidently developing his system, even to bringing non-Aryan myths within the solar formula, Lang entered his objections in the first number for 1886, in a brisk piece on "Myths and Mythologists."[16]

Pushing forward his examination of "savage" myths and tales, Lang produced his most substantial work in the field of mythology and folklore in 1887 with his two-volume study, *Myth, Ritual, and Religion.* Here he amassed world-wide evidence to support his contention that primitive peoples everywhere possessed similar beliefs, tales, and customs, which survived in classic Greek myths and in modern peasant lore. This exposition powerfully influenced the new generation of folklorists who had in 1878 formed a Folk-Lore Society and initiated a folklore journal. Following Müller's exhaustive rebuttal in his *Science of Comparative Mythology,* Lang replied the same year (1897) with a point-by-point rejoinder in *Modern Mythology.* Curiously, also in this year, the last and most intense of their public disagreement, Lang visited Müller at Norham Gardens, and subsequently they exchanged cordial letters.[17]

Numerous other figures entered into the mythological controversy before, during, and after the debate just outlined. In a lecture delivered before the Royal Institution in 1871, Müller rose to a greater heat of anger than he ever displayed against Lang, for the smashing denunciation of comparative mythology uttered in that very room a year before by the Greek scholar, John Stuart Blackie.[18] Both Müller and Cox fought a rearguard action with the Right Honorable William E. Gladstone, who insisted on interpreting Greek myths as a degraded form of Revelation. Robert Brown refuted Lang's refutation of Müller's *Science of Comparative Mythology* with his own book of jibes and sneers, which elicited a smoking retort from Lang. Müller and Lang joined hands in pouncing on the mythological innovations of Herbert Spencer, who ascribed the beginnings of myths to savage worship of ancestors. Then they fell to arguing whether Mannhardt in Germany, Tiele in Holland, Canizzaro or Morselli in Italy, Gaidoz in France, and Horatio Hale in the United States supported the philological or ethnological position. But these sideshows merely heightened interest in the main event.

Max Müller arrived at his solar interpretation of myths through comparative philology. He tells in his autobiography of his exhilaration in turning from classical studies to the novelties of Sanscrit; he heard Klee and Brockhaus at the University of Leipzig in the years 1838 to 1841 with the sense of peering into the dawn of civilization.[19] His fascination for Sanscrit took him to Berlin in 1844 to hear Bopp, a founder of comparative philology, to Paris the next year to collate Sanscrit manuscripts under the direction of Burnouf, and to London in 1846 to seek the patronage of the East India Company in publishing a projected translation of the Rig-Veda. Müller candidly reveals in later life what a priggish bookworm he was when a stripling in Paris, sleeping one night out of three and starving himself to continue his studies, with never a thought for society or gaiety. But at twenty-three he had found his life's work, the study of the ancient literature of India, and his master thesis, that the religion, the thought, the language, and the mythology of the Aryan people could be unveiled from the Vedas.[20]

Both Müller and Lang puzzled over an anomaly no scholar had yet explained, the barbarous elements in Greek myths.

How could so civilized a people repeat such degrading stories about their gods? The mystery can be cleared up, Müller reasons, by tracing the names of the Greek deities to their Sanscrit equivalents, and then reading in the Veda, the oldest literary monument of the Aryan peoples, to perceive the true nature of the gods. All the Indo-European peoples belonged to a common Aryan stock; after the migration of the European groups from their Indic homeland, the parent language, and the mythology it related, splintered into various off-shoots. A time came when the original meanings of the names of the Vedic gods were forgotten, and survived only in mythical phrases and proverbs of uncertain sense. Stories then developed to explain these phrases. From this "disease of language" myths were born.

Müller postulated a "mythopoeic" age when truly noble conceptions of the Aryan gods first arose. This age occurred, not at the beginning of civilization, but at a stage early enough so that language could not convey abstract notions. Two processes developed to carry the burden of communication: polyonymy, where one word carried many meanings, and homonymy, where one idea became attached to different words. Dyaus, the supreme god, might be understood as sky, sun, air, dawn, light, brightness. Conversely, a number of different words might signify the sun, with its complex of associations. These phenomena of mythopoeic thought and speech thickened the confusion resulting from the "disease of language."

Metaphors thus operated in two ways. The same verb root, for instance "to shine," could form the name of the sun or a term for the brightness of thought. Then again, nouns so formed could be transferred poetically to other objects; the rays of the sun become fingers, clouds are called mountains, the rain-clouds are referred to as cows with heavy udders, the lightning receives the appellation arrow or serpent. These metaphorical words are "Appellatives," and form the substance of myths.[21] Müller always stressed that solar interpretation must be based on strict phonetic rules. The "ponderous squibs" that had reduced the nursery song of sixpence, or Napoleon, or a gentleman named Mr. Bright, or Max Müller himself, to solar myths, all went wide of the mark in ridiculing the excesses of comparative mythologists who failed to *identify* similar gods and heroes with etymological proofs.[22]

Clearly, mythopoeic man constructed his pantheon around the sun, the dawn, and the sky. How could it be otherwise?, Müller asked. "What we call the Morning, the ancient Aryans called the Sun or the Dawn . . . What we call Noon, and Evening, and Night, what we call Spring and Winter, what we call Year, and Time, and Life, and Eternity—all this the ancient Aryans called *Sun*. And yet wise people wonder and say, How curious that the ancient Aryans should have had so many solar myths. Why, every time we say 'Good morning,' we commit a solar myth. Every poet who sings about 'the May driving the Winter from the field again' commits a solar myth. Every 'Christmas number' of our newspapers—ringing out the old year and ringing in the new—is brimful of solar myths. Be not afraid of solar myths . . . ."[23]

The major triumph of comparative mythology lay in the equation Dyaus=Zeus, which associated the supreme gods of the Greeks and Vedic pantheons. If they were identical, their families of lesser gods and goddesses must equally be kin. Dyaus is the Vedic sky-god, and now the ugly mystery of the Greek myth of Cronus and Zeus is cleared up. Cronus castrated his father, Uranus, at the behest of his mother, Gaea, who was both Uranus's wife and daughter. Cronus then married his own sister and swallowed his children as fast as they were born. But Zeus escaped when his mother substituted for him a stone swaddled like a baby. Then Zeus compelled Cronus to disgorge his brothers and sisters. Scarcely a fitting tale to introduce the beauties of Greek mythology to the younger generation! But now we see plainly that the marriage of Uranus and Gaea represents the union of Heaven and Earth. The paternal cannibalism of Cronus originally signified the heavens devouring and later releasing, the clouds, and the act of Zeus depicts the final separation of Heaven and Earth, and the commencement of man's history.[24]

In making their equations, Müller and other comparative philologists of his day filled their pages with a series of acrostic puzzles that inevitably arrived, after conjecture, surmise, and supposition, at a predestined goal. For Müller it was the sun, for Kuhn the storm-clouds, for Schwartz the wind, for Preller the sky.[25] With increasing acerbity Müller told Lang and all non-Sanscritists to stay out of these arguments,[26] but on occasion he did provide English readers with homely examples of the "forgetfulness of language," which he dubbed "modern mythology." The arms of Oxford, displaying an ox crossing a ford, represented such a popular etymology. Look how "cocoa" has absorbed "cacao," how "God" is associated with "good," how "lark," as sport, suggests the bird. We speak of "swallowing" one's pride, and perhaps an early swallower was named Cronus.[27] One dramatic illustration that Müller offered to clinch his point dealt with the modern myth of the barnacle goose, reported by sailors and travelers who had seen birds hatched from shellfish. Working back in time through his sources, Müller eventually arrived at a twelfth century Irish version from Giraldus Cambrensis. Then he gives the key. Irish birds would be called Hiberniculae, a name eventually shortened to Berniculae, which easily becomes Bernacula, and is confused with "barnacles." In this way linguistic confusion creates the myth of birds being born from barnacles. Similarly, speculates Müller, the legend of Dick Whittington and his cat could have arisen from misapprehension of the French "achat," trade, to which Whittington actually owed his wealth, but which in English was rendered "a cat."[28] Unravel this kind of verbal confusion, and the puzzling elements in Greek myths appear as legends springing up around divine names which, before the Aryan separation, signified the sun and the dawn.

Andrew Lang read the classics at Oxford in the years just after the bombshell of Darwin burst over the Western world. The theory of biological evolution led logically into the hypothesis of human evolution, so it seemed in the dazzling researches of Edward B. Tylor, whom Lang always cites with reverence. The major works of Tylor appeared in 1865 and 1871, at the very outset of Lang's career, and set his mind in the path of evolutionary anthropology, with a conviction equal to Müller's faith in comparative philology. Confounded, like Müller, by the irrational and brutal aspects of Greek myths, Lang moved naturally from his early Homeric studies into the realm of mythology and folklore. His system began with the premise that the history of mankind followed a uniform development from savagery to civilization, and that relics of primitive belief and custom survived still among the rural peasantry, and among contemporary savages. These relics, or "survivals," could assist in reconstructing the earliest stages of human life and culture, much as the fossil bones of a prehistoric creature could conjure up an extinct species. Previous evidence secured from travelers and missionaries, and new testimony steadily being gathered by conscientious collectors, offered a mass of data on the traditions of savages and peasants. Everywhere the same beliefs, and survivals of beliefs, manifested themselves; primitive man ascribed spirits to the trees, the animals, and the elements, he worshipped the animal protector of his clan, he credited the shaman with powers of transformation. Myths and fairy tales continually reveal the concepts of animism, totemism, fetishism, for they hark back to the stage of culture when men did not sharply distinguish between the human and the natural world. Collections of savage folktales and rural folklore demonstrate the continued credence in metamorphosis and other magic. So there is nothing surprising in the myth of Cronus, which obviously dates from an era of cannibalism. Aryan traditions can only be understood through comparison with non-Aryan myths and legends the world over. We learn about Greek gods from red Indian totems.[29]

No compromise could reconcile two such widely divergent theories, and Lang promptly turned his cunning scalpel into Müller's delicate hypotheses. Again and again he pointed to the disagreements among the experts on the Greek-Vedic equations, the cornerstone of Müller's edifice. Then he asked embarrassing questions. Since all primitive men have myths, why did not myths originate before the Mythopoeic Age? Why would mythopoeic man remember phrases and forget their meanings? Why does Müller devise the cumbersome processes of polyonymy and homonymy to explain a very simple phenomenon, namely, that savages regarded the elements as persons? Lang pointed out possibilities for error within the etymological method: antique legends could gravitate to modern heroes whose names would merely mislead the inquirer; names for elements were often taken by savages (as among the red Indians), and would again produce false scents.[30] Folk etymologies exist, of course, but mainly in connection with *place-names*.[31] In any case, how can Comparative Mythology explain the myths of non-Aryan races, lower in culture than the Vedic Aryans, unacquainted with Sanscrit, yet possessing legends similar to those found in India and Greece?

Lang never denied the presence of solar myths, and lunar and star myths as well, and offered copious examples in his *Myth, Ritual, and Religion*. They issue, he reiterated, not from any "disease of language" but from the animistic stage of culture, which personalized the elements and accepted metamorphosis. Thus the mythical Zeus has "all the powers of the medicine-man and all the passions of the barbarian."[32] Relentlessly Lang bombarded the solar mythologists with examples from Australia, Africa, North and South America, and the south Pacific islands of savage traditions that resembled those of civilized peoples. The believed tales of primitive culture survive in the myths and *Märchen* of a later day, and account for their odd features. "It is almost as necessary for a young god or hero to slay monsters as for a young lady to be presented at court; and we may hesitate to explain all these legends of an useful feat of courage as nature-myths."[33] Where Müller and his followers invariably interpreted the hero vanquishing the dragon as the sun conquering the night, Lang saw an ancient storytelling formula.

Müller never conceded an inch. He stuck fast to his etymologies, and berated Lang for discussing Sanscrit matters on which he was ignorant. However, he dissociated himself from any conclusions not based on the identifications of Greek and Sanscrit proper names, and considered his follower Cox unwary for submitting proofs based solely on analogies.[34] While Lang never learned Sanscrit, his opponent increasingly considered ethnological materials. Further, Müller strongly counterattacked the ethnological position, and criticized the ambiguities and convenient vagueness of such terms as totemism, animism, fetishism, and savages.[35] He disparaged the data obtained from savages by missionaries and travelers as credulous, biased, and colored by public opinion and priestly authority, and demanded that observers master the native languages.[36] (English anthropologists today criticize their American colleagues for not learning languages.) Are all savages alike? he asked, and answered that further study of savage myths and customs would reveal more contradictions than ever the philologists brewed, "with this important difference, that scholars can judge of etymologies by themselves, while many a Baron Munchhausen escapes entirely from our cross-examination."[37] Think what a hodge-podge of creeds and customs a curious Finn would find in England, especially if he had to rely on interpreters! Unless the motive is the same in each case, the customs extracted from different cultures are not true analogies.[38]

So Müller anticipated the lethal shafts modern anthropology would direct at comparative ethnologists such as Frazer. For totemism he reserved his choicest barbs. Totems conveniently appeared wherever the ethnologist found some belief or rite involving an animal. Should Müller's friend, Abeken, whose name means small ape, and who displays an ape in his coat of arms, be assigned the ape as his totem? "It is true I never saw him eating an ape, but I feel certain this was not from any regard for his supposed ancestor or totem, but was with him a mere matter of taste."[39] What does animism and totemism explain, in any event? To say that the myth of Daphne can be understood because Samoans and Sarawakians believed women could change into trees is to explain *ignotum per ignotius;* why would they believe such a thing?[40] Müller thus threw back at Lang his charge that philology failed to account for the nasty and senseless stories about Greek gods.

Far from abandoning his philological "fortress," Müller sallied forth to annex folklore territory. The ethno-psychological school shared his objectives, and he would gladly work with them, provided they observed proper scholarly caution and learned languages.[41] Müller stoutly asserted his friendship for ethnology. He spoke warmly of Tylor, whose *Researches into the Early History of Mankind* he reviewed sympathetically, but with the admonition that the comparison of customs should keep within the bounds of comparative languages.[42] Indeed, he quoted "My friend, Mr. Tylor," in support of solar mythology, and for evidence on the unreli-

ability of travelers' reports.[43] Müller himself had strenuously
pleaded for the establishment of an archives on "Ethnological
Records of the English Colonies," recognizing the great opportunity afforded by the dominions, colonies, and missionary
societies of the British Empire, but the project was allowed
to languish.[44] He had once compiled a Mohawk grammar,
and would certainly learn savage tongues if time permitted.[45]
Since life was finite, he must rely on scholarly missionaries
who had themselves translated the tales of primitive peoples;
and so he consulted closely with Patteson, Codrington, and
Gill on Melanesian and Polynesian dialects, with Bleek and
Hahn on African folklore, and with Horatio Hale on American Indian dialects.[46] He knew the work of Rev. J. S. Whit-
mee, who hoped to collect "choice myths and songs" that
would make possible a comparative study of Polynesian
mythology.[47] And he supplied a preface for the book of traditions brought back from the island of Mangaia by the Rev.
W. Wyatt Gill, in which he pointed eagerly to this record of
mythopoeic men who believe in gods and offer them human
sacrifices.[48] In 1891 the Oxford don served as president of
the Ethnological Section of the British Association.[49]

The modern reader of Max Müller's mythological theory
may find himself astonished at the sophistication of the Sanscrit scholar in matters ethnological. With startling insight he
dissected the stereotyped notion of a "savage," to show how
the qualities imputed to him applied just as readily to the
civilized man. "When we read some of the more recent works
on anthropology, the primordial savage seems to be not unlike one of those hideous india-rubber dolls that can be
squeezed into every possible shape, and made to utter every
possible noise. . . ."[50] Contemporary "savages" have lived as
long as civilized races, and are nothing like primitive man.
Actually the Andaman Islanders enjoyed a felicitous existence that a European laborer would gladly embrace.[51]

Then, after playfully juxtaposing the contradictory reports
about savages, which reveal only the ignorance of the be-
holders, Müller does an unexpected turnabout. In an article
entitled "Solar Myths," he relies exclusively on "scholarlike"
ethnologists to support his thesis. Almost in the words of
Lang, he speaks about "the surprising coincidence in the folk-

lore, the superstitions and customs of the most remore races,"
and proceeds to explore this mystery. He finds that among the
non-Aryan peoples also, the trail always leads back through
the disease of language to a solar myth. Legends of the Polynesian Maui become intelligible when we recognize that his
name signifies the sun, or fire, or the day; the Hottentot deity
Tsui-goab, now understood as Broken-Knee, originally meant
the red dawn or the rising sun; Michabo, the Great Hare of
the Algonkins, can be traced back to the god of Light. So,
thanks to the ethnological school of comparative mythology,
the preoccupation of early man everywhere with the life-
giving sun, about which he spun his legends and riddles and
myths, becomes manifest.[52]

In his books too Müller compares crude New Zealand
origin tales with Greek myths, and juxtaposes the Polynesian
Maui with gods of the Veda, in the manner of Lang, but in
the interests of solarism.[53] The *Kalevala* fascinated him as
much as the Scot, and he corresponded with Krohn about
Finnish folklore.[54] Like the most confirmed ethno-folklorist,
he culled myths from the Eskimos, the Hottentots, and the
Esthonians, to illustrate the male and female personifications
of sun, moon, and stars already known from his Aryan examples.[55] He produces superstitious customs of Scottish,
Irish, and German peasants, which acquire a mythological
hue.[56] And he makes a vigorous plea for the methods of comparative folklore in studying mythology, before Lang had
ever published a full-scale attack on his system.[57] Reading
these comments, one recognizes that Lang was often pillory-
ing a straw man—as Müller protested.[58]

In comparing non-Aryan with Aryan myths, Müller remained ever faithful to philological principles and the solar
viewpoint. If myths had degenerated into heroic legends, and
these into nursery tales, the reflection of the sun still shone,
even in Red Riding Hood and Cinderella, and perhaps could
be retraced etymologically.[59] He praised the ethnological
work of Lewis Morgan and John Wesley Powell in the United
States, based entirely on linguistics, and pointed trium-
phantly to the etymology for Gitse-Manito whose root, "to
warm," clearly led back to the sun.[60] Müller's own inquiries
into Mordvinian myths, relying on collections made by lin-

guistic scholars, revealed the same solar origins he had traced for Vedic gods. When Letts spoke of the golden boat that sinks into the sea, or the apple that falls from the tree, they referred unwittingly to the setting sun.[61]

At the end of the long debate, it was Lang who gave ground. *Modern Mythology* finds him curiously on the defensive, qualifying his position on totemism, and admitting the differences between himself and Frazer on totemic survivals. Instead of referring to Samoan "totems," Lang will henceforth speak of Samoan "sacred animals," as more exact, since to prove sacred beasts are totems requires definite evidence.[62] In revising his *Myth, Ritual, and Religion,* in 1899, Lang made such extensive concessions that Hartland, who reviewed the new edition in *Folk-Lore,* the organ of the anthropological school, averred Lang had delivered himself into his opponents' hands.[63] Speculating on religious origins, Lang came to accept, on the basis of anthropological evidence, the same conception of "high gods" and pure spiritual ideas among primitive peoples that Müller supported intuitively and philosophically. Lang challenged Tylor on the animistic origins of religious belief, and ceased to present the upward ascent of man as a clear-cut evolutionary climb.[64] In his new edition he added the sentence, "The lowest savagery scarcely ever, if ever, wholly loses sight of a heavenly father," after the statement, "The most brilliant civilization of the world never expelled the old savage from its myth and ritual." Again, he appends two new sentences to his chapter on "Mexican Divine Myths" to soften the original conclusion that even the Spanish Inquisition advanced over barbarous Mexican ritual. The new ending holds that wild polytheistic myths grow around gods unknown to low savage races, who recognize a "moral primal Being."[65] In asserting the Godliness of early man, Lang elevates the savage mentality, and so injures his thesis that survivals or borrowings from savages explain the irrational elements in myths and fairy tales.

The solar theory was carried to lengths far exceeding the etymological boundaries of Max Müller by his most aggressive disciple, George William Cox. An Oxford graduate, clergyman, self-styled baronet (his claim was posthumously denied), and a popular writer on Greek history and mythology, Cox developed what his master called the "analogical" school of comparative mythology. He presented this viewpoint first in conventional retellings of classical myths, *Tales from Greek Mythology* (1861), and *Tales of the Gods and Heroes* (1862),[66] then in a deceptive *Manual of Mythology* (1867), which by a series of leading questions and loaded answers converted innocent school children to solarism, until finally he engulfed the adult reading public with two large volumes on *The Mythology of the Aryan Nations* (1870), and *An Introduction to the Science of Comparative Mythology and Folklore* (1881). Throughout these writings Cox quotes, cites, and invokes the name of Max Müller on nearly every page, and reduces all Aryan myths, legends, and fairy tales to the contest between sun and night. Müller's "Essay on Comparative Mythology" first charmed him into a field previously "repulsive." Building on that solid foundation he had completely reconstructed the original mythology of India and Greece, through one new insight: the resemblance of all Aryan narratives to each other. Max Müller had demonstrated by etymological proofs the identity of certain Homeric and Vedic gods, and their common origin, through "failure of memory" (which Cox preferred to "disease of language"), in phrases about the sun. Now Sir George will interpret the meaning of myths and legends which defied philological assault, through the comparison of their narrative elements.[67] By this method, the striking fact became apparent that every Greek hero performed the same feats, be he Achilles, Odysseus, Heracles, Theseus, Bellerophon, Appollon, Meleagros, or even Paris. Where his master regarded Paris as the night, Cox saw in him aspects of both night and day; Paris begins his career as a power of darkness, but ends as a solar deity.[68] Continually Cox called attention to the similarities in the legends of heroes, to their spears and arrows and invincible darts which represented the rays of the sun, to their wonderful steeds and magic swords. All their adventures follow the same pattern of a long Westward journey filled with labors and struggles, and this is the course of the daily sun. "The story of the sun starting in weakness and ending in victory, waging a long warfare against darkness, clouds, and storms, and scattering them all in the end, is the story of all patient self-sacrifice, of all Christian devotion."[69] The Achilleus is a splendid solar epic, portraying the contest between sun and night, and reaching its climax when Achilles tramples on the blood of his enemies as the glorious sun tramples out the dark clouds.[70]

Sir George of course had no patience with euhemerism. He blasted the article in the eighth edition of the *Encyclopaedia Britannica* asserting the historicity of heroes, and denied all factual basis for the saga of Grettir or the cycle of King Arthur, or any other solar hero. Four-fifths of the folklore of Northern Europe he swept into his solar net. Legends of death are blood-stained sunsets; stupid demons and ogres are the dark powers who must be conquered by light-born heroes; the episodes of heroes hidden in caves reflect the waxing and waning year.[71] Sigurd, William Tell, Roland, the Biblical David, all tell the same tale (and in his last mythological study Cox annexed Beowulf and Hamlet).[72] The fairy tales too conform to the elemental pattern. All the humble heroes who find riches and conquer dragons, whether Boots or the frog prince or Cinderella, are solar deities; Hansel and Gretel are dawn-children, and the ubiquitous gold that rewards the valiant hero is the golden light of the sun.[73] Under Cox's solar touch black becomes white, for the name of the horse "Black" can signify light and whiteness, as befits the steed of a solar hero.[74] Small wonder that Max Müller confessed dizziness at viewing this solar empire he had innocently opened up.[75]

Certain insights in Cox's work show a growing sophistication toward folklore. His extension of Müller's etymological equations into the area of structural comparisons was actually moving onto the sounder ground of type and motif analysis. The great heroes of epic and legend do betray astonishing resemblances, which have evoked the historical thesis of the Chadwicks, that comparable periods of cultural history produce an "Heroic Age," and the ritual-origins theory popularized by Lord Raglan, who substitutes the dying and reborn god for the waning and waxing sun. Cox recognized common elements in myths, legends, and *Märchen*, and understood more perceptively than Müller that a cluster of incidents hangs together to form a folktale com-

plex. He pointed out that Müller had confused a fable in the
Hitopadesa with the Master Thief, and commented, "The
possible affinity of thievish stratagems in all countries can
scarcely account for a series of extraordinary incidents and
astounding tricks following each other in the same order, although utterly different in their outward garb and color-
ing."[76] He himself then confused the Master Thief with the
legend of Rhampsinitus.[77] To protect his pan-Aryan theory,
Cox had to deny the possibility that solar legends spread by
borrowing, and obtusely contended that the greater the resemblance, the less the chance for diffusion! He conceived of
borrowing in purely literary terms, and argued that a borrowed tale must perfectly match its original. Similar but not
identical narratives indicate a common source, in Vedic
India.[78] Mythology and folklore converge in Cox's solarism,
and he claimed as their only distinction the possibility of sub-
jecting a myth to philological analysis.[79]

In his well-known introduction to the Hunt edition of
Grimm's *Household Tales,* Lang dealt at length with the
theories of Sir George, and in some perplexity. The edge of
his wit was turned by the unpredictable departure of the
pupil from his master, for on some points Cox veered so
abruptly from Max Müller that he landed squarely in Lang's
arms. When Sir George posited an animistic state of savagery
conducive to mythmaking, and conceived that animistic ideas
grew from savage thought, not from confused language, Lang
naturally applauded. The foe of solarism approved the way
Cox refused to trace myths merely through names, as Müller
demanded, and he supported Cox's view that *Märchen* can be
both the remains and the sources of myth.[80]

A mystified Lang could not see how Sir George, quoting
Müller chapter and verse, drew inferences congenial to the
anthropological viewpoint. Cox should have gone to the evidence about savage customs and ideas, not to the philologists,
Lang said, and then his correct inferences might have led to
correct conclusions. Unfortunately, those conclusions echoed
Müller's, in reading the sun and the clouds and the dew into
every myth and tale, and Lang mocked the two solarists im-
partially when he came to analyze their reconstructions. He
laughed polyonymy and the forgetfulness-of-words into the

ground, as he attempted by these processes to explain the Jason myth, and then he showed how simply the anthropologists could decipher the story. But Cox never became the *bête noire* to Lang that Müller was, and the Scot may have considered that, born a bit later, Sir George would have found the right tutor.[81]

No adversary in the camp of the comparative mythologists smarted from Lang's barbs with such pain as Robert Brown, Junior, of Barton-on-Humber. Brown labored manfully during the 1870's and '80's to establish the influence of the ancient Semitic cultures on Hellenic religious mythology. Invitingly he wrote, "he who is wearied with the familiar aroma of the Aryan field of research may stimulate and refresh his jaded senses with new perfumes wafted from the shores of the Euphrates and the Nile."[82] As Max Müller sought to draw the Greek pantheon into the folds of Vedic conceptions, so Robert Brown, the Assyriologist and Egyptologist, attempted to clasp Hellas within the orbit of Near Eastern cults and myths. Comparative mythology had launched a powerful pincers movement on classical Greece, from India and from Egypt, which bid fair to rob Athens of most claims to originality. If Müller demanded that mythologists study Sanscrit, and Lang insisted they read ethnology, Brown declared they must acquaint themselves with the latest research on Chaldea, Assyria, Phoenicia, Arabia, Persia, and Egypt. Semitic Asia had contributed at least as many divinities to the Greek pantheon as had Aryan India![83] The extent of these contributions Brown measured in studies of *Poseidôn* (1872), *The Great Dionysiak Myth*, 2 vols. (1877-1878), *The Unicorn* (1881), and *The Myth of Kirkê* (1883), and summarized his position, in the face of Lang's taunts, in *Semitic Influence in Hellenic Mythology* (1898).[84]

Although this last work originated as a rebuttal to *Modern Mythology*, Brown by no means slavishly followed Müller and Cox. His Semitic bias naturally led him into differences with the Vedic scholar, whose school he criticized for excessive pan-Aryanism.[85] Cox, rather than Müller, dominates his footnotes, however, and the "Aryo-Semitic" mythologist steadily refers to the interpretations in *The Mythology of the Aryan Nations*, with due respect to its author (who returned the compliments), but with cavils at his neglect of Semitic gods.[86] Brown's thesis compelled him to grant some historical basis to legends, in spite of all the harsh words then accorded euhemerism, for he necessarily supported his arguments with geographical and historical facts of commerce, travel, and migration throughout the Aegean area. Cox and Müller laughed away all history behind myth, secure in the one historical point that Aryan peoples emigrated from India and carried their language and myths with them; but Brown had to demonstrate that physical contact, not an ancient linguistic inheritance, gave Greek deities a Semitic gloss. Art and arch-aeology documented his position, and clothed the bare bones of philology.[87] Therefore, he called into evidence the Egyp-tian character of a splendid belt worn by Heracles, or the Phoenician skill at packaging reflected in the "curious knot" Circe taught Odysseus how to tie.[88] To show his eclecticism, Brown scoffed at some excesses of the "Natural Phenomena Theory."[89] How could Polyphemos be the eye of the sun, blinded by the solar hero Odysseus, for would the sun blind himself? How could Skeiron, the wind, be first slain and then devoured by a tortoise?[90]

Most of Brown's explications, however, conform to rigid solar orthodoxy. The trip of Odysseus to the underworld represents the span of a day and a night, during which the sun descends beyond the horizon, and all the mythical figures the solar hero meets in the depths are also solar characters: Tityos stretched on the ground attacked by two vultures is the sun besieged by the powers of darkness; Tantalos reach-ing for water that always recedes is the suffering sun, and so is Sisyphos, trying vainly to push a solar stone over the brow of the hill that is heaven, and so of course is Heracles, draw-ing his bow in the midst of the dead. Thus the dead sun suf-fers every night.[91] Throughout the massive data on Dionysos the solar character of the complex divinity predominates. One myth associated with his name has a lion chase a leopard into a cave; the leopard emerges from another entrance, re-enters the cave and devours the lion, who has been caught fast, from behind. Here the lion is the flaming sun, and the cave and the leopard are both the dark night; night mounts into heaven behind the hidden sun and gnaws him to death—

although he will be reborn at the East portal next morning.[92] No narrow solar mythologist, Brown displayed lunar and stellar sympathies, and analyzed the Unicorn as "the wild, white, fierce, chaste Moon," and Circe as the moon-goddess beloved by the solar Heracles. Medusa is the "Serpentine-full-moon, the victim of the solar Perseus," and her petrifying stare signifies the moon-glare of a soundless night.[93]

On every occasion Brown reasserted the Semitic provenience of gods and myths found in Greece. After following the trail of Dionysos through the poets and dramatists and cults, in gems and vases and epithets, Brown placed the origin of the vast complex in Chaldea. "Here, then, is Dumuzi-Tammuz on Assyrian and Kaldean ground, side by side, and in truth identical with Dian-nisi-Dionysos, the judge-of-men, the ruling, judging, sinking, life-giving, all-sustaining Sun, diurnal and nocturnal . . . ."[94] As the myth traveled Westward across the Aegean, Hellenic culture softened some of its wilder orgiastic features, although traces remained in the Eleusinian mysteries. The sea-god Poseidôn too originated in Chaldea, and entered Greece through Phoenicia and Libya; he resembles the Biblical Noah and the Chaldean Oannês, a creature that rose out of the sea and instructed men in the arts and letters.[95] An Egyptian papyrus of the twelfth Dynasty first presents in mythical form the great solar voyage across heaven, as the tale of an archaic sea-captain who visited the land of shadows.[96] From such data, Brown felt justified in capping the debate between Lang and Müller with the formation of the new Aryo-Semitic school of comparative mythology.[97]

Lacking the sparkle of Lang and the limpid style of Müller, Brown appears at a disadvantage when he comes fuming into the controversy. His antiquarian volumes are filled with rejoinders to dead authorities, classical quotations, genealogical tables of deities, philological equations, and the accumulation of recondite evidence more or less germane to the inquiry. In *Semitic Influence in Hellenic Mythology* Brown tried to match Lang at his own game of taunt and gibe, not without some trepidation in tackling an opponent who might have given pause to Heracles himself. Brown and Müller both complained that Lang's numerous journalistic outlets,

daily, weekly, and monthly, gave him opportunity to throw
up an artificial cloud of scorn over solar mythology.[98] Now
the Egyptologist bitterly accused Lang of misrepresenting
himself, Müller, and Cox; he pointed to the world-wide evidence for solar myths (which Lang never denied), and attacked the theory of totemism and survivals on the grounds
that Hellenic constellation-names and legends derive from
the advanced civilization of the Phoenicians.[99] If philologists
disagree, one can still be right; and they do agree on the
general outlines of the Natural Phenomena Theory. The
intense pique of Brown emerges on nearly every page, and
produces a curious appendix, entitled "Professor Agucheki-
kos On Totemism," intended as a *jeu d'esprit* paraphrasing
the anti-solar arguments of Lang himself. The satire purports
to be a review written in 4886 A.D. of a learned study on
Anglican Totemism in the Victorian Epoch, which infers the
prevalence of totemism from the animal names of clans, such
as the Bulls and the Bears, who once struggled in a "stock
exchange," and from such archaic expressions as calling a
man "a snake in the grass."[100]

Although Lang flicked Robert Brown with the same whip
he used on all his adversaries, including his friends, on this
victim he drew the most blood. Brown refers furiously to an
anonymous review of *The Myth of Kirkê* in the *Saturday
Review,* obviously by Lang, where the Scot had ridiculed
the solar theory, saying that Robinson Crusoe, like Odysseus,
lived in a cave, and so must be the sun. A debate ensued in
the *Academy,* in which, "according to general opinion the
brilliant journalist came off but second best."[101] In *Custom
and Myth* Lang called the views elaborated by Brown in *The
Law of Kosmic Order,* that the Accadians named the stars
after celestial myths, "far-fetched and unconvincing." Even
granting that the Greeks obtained their star-names from
Chaldea, did the Eskimos and Melanesians name stars after
Accadian fancies? The Accadians too must have inherited
beliefs from a savage past, which they used in naming the
constellations.[102] In another chapter Lang dealt with Brown's
analysis of the magic herb moly, given Odysseus to ward off
the spells of Circe. Brown construed moly as originally a
star, known to the ancient Accadians, that guarded a solar

hero; Lang thought it simply a magical herb of the kind everywhere credited by savages. He quotes Brown in the *Academy* for 3 January 1885, as contending that "if Odysseus and Kirkê were sun and moon here is a good starting-point for the theory that the moly was stellar." Then he inserted the lance. "This reminds one of the preacher who demonstrated the existence of the Trinity thus: 'For is there not, my brethren, one sun, and one moon,—and one multitude of stars?' "[103] The Accadian theory, he sighs, is becoming as overdone as the Aryan. In a preface to a new edition of *Custom and Myth* (1898), Lang replied to Brown's attack earlier that year with blistering severity.[104]

A word must be given to the massive two-volume work on *Zoological Mythology, or The Legends of Animals,* by Angelo De Gubernatis, which appeared in 1872. The Italian professor of Sanscrit published this work in English as a tribute, no doubt, to the reputation of Max Müller and the lively interest in England in Comparative Mythology. Ruefully the author remarked, "It has fallen to me to study the least elevated department of mythology,"[105] the appearance of gods in animal forms, assumed when they broke a taboo, or served a term of punishment. A vast body of popular lore now described the actions of Aryan gods in animal disguises, where formerly they had appeared as celestial phenomena. Beginning with myths about the sacred bull and cows of the Rigvedas, who represent the sun-god Indras and the clouds, Gubernatis moved to Slavonic and other European parallel tales, and then systematically considered further beasts recurring in *Märchen,* in the usual solar terms. The soul of the ass is the sun; the whale is the night; the peacock is the starry sky; the crab is the moon; birds of prey are lightning and thunderbolts; the serpent-devil is the power of darkness.[106] In Jack and the Beanstalk, Jack's mother is the blind cow, that is, the darkened aurora; she scatters beans, and the bean of abundance, which is the moon, grows up to the sky; this Jack climbs to the wealth of the morning light.[107] Gubernatis necessarily brought many folktales within his net, and recognized some kinships; for instance, he discerned the tale-type of the man or animal trapped by putting his hands or paws in the cleft of a tree trunk,[108] and he uncovered the legend of the

peasant who overheard the talking bulls on Christmas eve
prophesy his own death.[109]

The mythological disputants of the period continually refer
to this zoological compendium. Brown praised Gubernatis
for recognizing the solar character of the hog,[110] and Lang
scoffed at him for interpreting the cat as the moon and the
mouse as the shadows of night. How, when the moon-cat is
away, can there be any light to make playful mice-shad-
ows?[111] Even the sympathetic reviewer in *The Scotsman*
complained that this overdose of celestial interpretations was
blunting his confidence in comparative mythology.[112]

The solar theory found strong support across the Atlantic
in the ethnologist Daniel Brinton, who wrote widely on
American Indian culture and language. In *The Myths of the
New World* (1868), a work reprinted for the remainder of
the century, Brinton compared the origin and creation myths
and culture-hero legends of North and South American
Indian tribes, to ascertain their inner meanings. The tropes of
language and the rites of worship offered him clues, and before long he had found the answer. "As the dawn brings light,
and with light is associated in every human mind the ideas
of knowledge, safety, protection, majesty, divinity, as it dis-
pels the spectres of night, as it defines the cardinal points,
and brings forth the sun and the day, it occupied the primitive mind to an extent that can hardly be magnified beyond
the truth."[113] Through the confusion of language, early man's
reactions to the dawn and the sun became transferred to animals or persons. Thus the Algonkin Michabo or Manabozho,
the Great Hare, comes from the root "wab," which means
both "rabbit" and "white," and in its latter sense originates
the words for the East, dawn, light, day, and morning. All
the legends about the Great Hare can easily be translated
into solar myths. Michabo is both the spirit of light who dis-
pels the darkness, and the lord of the winds. Degrading trickster stories associated with Michabo proceed from late and
corrupt versions of an inspiring mythology.[114]

Primeval man worshipped no brutes, but his own dim perception of the One, construed as lightness and whiteness.
Hence the first White men were regarded as gods. Brinton
was especially struck with the recurrence of the number

four in different tribal legends, and interpreted the four
demiurgic brothers as the four winds and the four cardinal
points. Declaring he was no slavish solar mythologist, Brinton proudly emphasized the attention he gave to the moon,
and the space he devoted to gods of thunderstorms and
lightning.[115]

Max Müller purred with delight on reading the pages of
this unexpected ally across the sea. Still licking his wounds
from the thrusts of Lang in 1884, the Oxford professor in his
article on "Solar Myths" the next year quoted gleefully long
passages from Brinton that illustrated the solar theory.
"When copying these lines," he marveled, "I felt almost as if
copying what I had written myself," and he was all the more
pleased because his own work "could in no way have influenced the conclusions of this eminent American writer."[116]
While Brinton quoted from Müller only once, on the Dawn
and the Sun,[117] he showed familiarity with the celestial theories of continental writers, and confidently asserted the parallels between Indian and European heavenly deities.[118]
Happily Müller underscored Brinton's contention that Indian
myths conformed to the world-view of early man everywhere, and in the etymology of "wab" he saw the Algonkin
counterpart of the Sanscrit root *div* or *dyu* that produced
Dyaus and Zeus.[119]

Replying in the very next issue of the *Nineteenth Century*,
Lang poured his vitriol on the Americanist. When there are
twenty known Algonkin totems, why does Brinton single out
the hare for his dubious etymology, and ignore the bear,
turtle, crane, wolf, coyote, and the others? All we know of
early Indian opinion directly contradicts this monotheistic
conception of the Great Hare—and supports, of course, totemism.[120] Lang failed to strike at a particularly vulnerable
spot in Brinton's argument, his exclusion of the trickster
aspect of Manabozho. Another weakness, Brinton's postulate
of the psychological unity of mankind, came too close to
Lang's own views for exposure, although where Lang saw
animism, Brinton perceived sun-worship. Irritatedly Lang
concludes, "Obviously there is not much to be learned by
trying to follow the curiously devious trail of Dr. Brinton
through the forest of mythology."[121]

The well-known American historian and evolutionist, John Fiske, also entered the arena of Comparative Mythology with one extremely popular book, *Myths and Myth-Makers* (1873), which ran through eleven editions in fifteen years. In a manner anticipating the pleasant discursiveness of Andrew Lang's *Custom and Myth*, Fiske rambled through the byways of folklore and mythology, to delineate his thesis from different angles. One essay treats the same topic that Lang considers, the divining rod, but where the Scot sees the rod as evidence of a surviving superstition, the American finds in it a representation of the lightning.[122] Fiske shows a remarkable acquaintance with the literature of both mythology and folklore, and quotes equally from the German philologists, the English solarists, ethnological collectors of primitive tales, including Brinton, and the British county fieldworkers, who rarely appear even in the citations of Lang. *Curious Myths of the Middle Ages,* produced by the unquenchable clergyman, Baring-Gould, especially stimulated his thought.

Fiske begins his essays like an orthodox solar mythologist. He explains away William Tell as a sun myth, views the historical Cyrus and Charlemagne as solar heroes, follows Cox on the dual aspect of Paris embracing both sun and night, and seeks to reconcile the storm-myths of Kuhn with the dawn-myths of Müller, as two aspects of the same interpretation.[123] The epic of the Iliad and the drama of Hamlet alike derive from primary myths about the sun, although Homer and Shakespeare never suspected the fact.[124]

A strange note nevertheless creeps into this conventional solar analysis. The petulant complaint that Cox overpresses his solar analogies seems but a passing mood, especially when the historian lashes at the euhemerism of Gladstone and Robert Brown.[125] But there is no mistaking Fiske's position by the time the final chapter is reached. For all his delight on first reading Müller's "Essay on Comparative Mythology," he sees carelessness and fallacies in its reasoning. The Sanscrit scholar has pressed the philological method into far greater service than it can render; other disciplines are needed to analyze myths, those of history (i.e., ethnology), and psychology. Müller has inverted the story of man's mythmaking;

metaphors came from myths, and not myths from diseased metaphors. A new mythmaking does invent later stories about gods and heroes whose original physical meanings are forgotten, and here lies the difference between the simple nature-myths of savages, and the more fanciful—and often inconsistent—tales of the Greeks. No confusion of language is involved, but merely the propensity of early man everywhere to build stories from his beliefs. "And in all countries may be found the beliefs that men may be changed into beasts, or plants, or stones; that the sun in some way tethered or constrained to follow a certain course; that the storm-cloud is a ravenous dragon; and that there are talismans which will reveal hidden treasures."[126] In the end Fiske quotes Tylor page after page, draws illustrations from primitive folklore, and postulates fetishism and animism as an early stage in the universal evolution of man. All this he does to refute the narrow philological approach of Müller, and to assert the ubiquity of solar myths from a more scientific point of view! John Fiske proves the reality of the Hegelian synthesis, for in his book the ideas of Lang and Müller intertwine like the rose and the briar.

With the death of Max Müller, in 1900, the cause of solar mythology lost its most lustrous name, and rapidly ebbed. When Lang revised his article on "Mythology" for the eleventh edition of the *Encyclopaedia Britannica* in 1911, he condensed his three columns of criticism on "The System of Max Müller" to a scanty half-column in small type, as a dead issue. Supplanting George W. Cox's *Introduction to the Science of Comparative Mythology and Folklore* came *An Introduction to Folk-Lore* (1895, new ed. 1905), by Marian Roalfe Cox, the disicple of Lang, Clodd, and Nutt, who faithfully follows the anthropological method. In the pamphlet series, "Popular Studies in Mythology, Romance and Folklore," designed for the general public, Sidney Hartland dealt with the topic *Mythology and Folktales: Their Relation and Interpretation* (1900), and buried the philological mythologists under the anthropological viewpoint. Hartland wrote that Lang had given the coup de grâce to comparative mythology in 1887 with his *Myth, Ritual, and Religion;*[127] but this statement ignores the subsequent writings of Müller and

Brown, and the modifications Hartland himself pointed out in the revised edition of *Myth, Ritual and Religion*. The eclipse of the solar theorists came in large part from the organization of the Folk-Lore Society in 1878, and the steady exposition in its journals and memoirs, and in the separate writings of its vigorous and prolific members, of the evolutionary interpretation. No Society of Comparative Mythology was formed.

One leaves a review of the great controversy with considerable respect for its protagonists. Müller emerges with scarcely less honor than Lang; the giants slew each other, although the corpse of cultural evolutionism bled more slowly than the dismembered torso of solarism. A spirit of fire and excitement vanished from the scene when the solar mythologists went under; Lang turned to fencing half-heartedly with his own colleagues, debating with Hartland over primitive religion, with Clodd about psychical research, and with Jacobs on the diffusion of tales, but he never rose to his earlier heights, or sustained so intense a campaign. One generation later when Lang and Hartland and Clodd had passed on, the Folk-Lore Society itself would become an outmoded survival, lacking direction or purpose or audience. But from 1856 to 1900 all England followed the battle between solar mythologists and "savage" folklorists. The new field collections were eagerly scanned upon their appearance, and pressed by the disputants into their respective dialectics. We envy the multiplicity of learned articles and books published, read, and bought in those literate Victorian days. And if we scorn the deluded theories of those embattled scholars,[128] let us remember that they had theories, based in erudition and presented with grace to an intellectually curious public absorbed in the furor concerning the early ideas of man.

NOTES

1. Stith Thompson, *The Folktale* (New York, 1946), pp. 371–375. The conventional view that Max Müller was a second-rate Victorian, slain by Lang's ethnology, is asserted by Richard

Chase, *Quest for Myth* (Baton Rouge, La., 1949), pp. 44-48, 58-65. Chase is unaware of Müller's interest in ethnology, and discusses the theories of myth held by Lang and Müller without any reference to the history of folklore, although they are inseparably connected. His ignorance of folklore leads him into the astonishing statement that Lang failed to show interest in folktales until late in life (pp. 61, 77). To Chase, myth is art, and he judges mythologists by his own prejudices.

2. Andrew Lang, "Max Müller," *Contemporary Review,* LXXVIII (1900), 785.

3. For the history of folklore theory, even in England, one must turn to European studies. There is gratifying detail on Müller and Lang in Giuseppe Cocchiara, *Storia del folklore in Europa* (Edizioni Scientifiche Einaudi, 1952), ch. 16, "Nel 'laboratorio' di Max Müller," pp. 309-324, and ch. 24, "Il primitivo che è in noi," pp. 461-469. A discussion of "Die Astralmythologie" appears in Åke Ohlmarks, *Heimdalls Horn und Odins Auge:* Erstes Buch (I-II), *Heimdallr und das Horn* (Lund and Kopenhagen, 1937), pp. 3-22, but the author fails to distinguish between religion and mythology in discussing Müller and Lang (pp. 6-8). Actually they rather agreed on the origin of religious ideas.

4. Georgina Max Müller, *The Life and Letters of the Right Honourable Friedrich Max Müller,* 2 vols. (New York, London, and Bombay, 1902), II, 7 and Appendix C, "Speech of Dean Liddell," 475-479.

5. Georgina Max Müller, *Life and Letters,* II, 452.

6. See *Concerning Andrew Lang,* Being the Andrew Lang Lectures delivered before the University of St. Andrews 1927-1937 (Oxford, 1949).

7. Roger L. Green has written *Andrew Lang, A Critical Biography,* with a Short-Title Bibliography of the Works of Andrew Lang (Leicester, Eng., 1946).

8. Fiske, *Myths and Myth-Makers* (Boston and New York, 1888), p. 209; Cox, *The Mythology of the Aryan Nations,* 2 vols. (London, 1870), I, v-vi; Lang, *Custom and Myth* (London, 1893), p. 58. Müller's essay was first published in *Oxford Essays* (1856) and reprinted in *Chips from a German Workshop,* II (London, 1867), 1-143. It was separately issued as *Comparative Mythology,* an essay edited with additional notes and an introductory preface on solar mythology by A. Smythe Palmer (London, 1909).

9. Thomas Sternberg, *The Dialect and Folk-Lore of Northamptonshire* (London, Northampton, Oundle, and Brackley, 1851).

10. Thomas Keightley, *The Mythology of Ancient Greece and Italy* (London, 1831).

11. This lecture was reprinted in Müller's *Selected Essays on Language, Mythology, and Religion,* I (London, 1881), along with other folkloristic essays previously published in *Chips, II,* and a lecture of 1870, "On the Migration of Fables."

12. Müller does not identify the review in his several repetitions of Lang's comment in *Contributions to the Science of Mythology,* 2 vols. (London, New York, and Bombay, 1897), I, 11, 32, 184. He does mention Lang, and only with praise, in articles in the *Nineteenth Century* on "The Savage," XVII (Jan., 1885), 117, and "Solar Myths," XVIII (Dec., 1885), 905.

13. Andrew Lang, *Modern Mythology* (London, 1897), pp. 3-4.

14. E.g., "Mr. Max Müller's Philosophy of Mythology," *Fraser's Magazine,* n.s. XXIV (August, 1881), 166-187, a detailed criticism of Müller's *Selected Essays;* and "Anthropology and the Vedas," *Folk-Lore Journal,* I (1883), 107-114, which disputes the idea in *Müller's Lectures on India, and what it can teach us* [sic] that the Vedas offer earlier information about mythological origins than do savage beliefs.

15. *La Mythologie,* traduit de l'anglais par Léon Parmentier, avec une préface par Charles Michel, et des additions de l'auteur (Paris, 1886). The book also included material from *Custom and Myth,* and Lang's article on "Prometheus" in the *Encyclopaedia Britannica.* The preface by Parmentier (v-xxxi) contains a useful resumé of the literature on comparative mythology. Lang gives interesting details on hearing Scottish "contes populaires" in his youth, and so being led into comparative folklore, in his preface (xxxv-xli).

16. Lang, "Myths and Mythologists," *Nineteenth Century,* XIX (Jan., 1886), 50-65. The force of Lang's rebuttal was diminished by a postscript Müller added to his article on "Solar Myths," *Nineteenth Century,* XVIII (Dec., 1885), 919-922, replying to a criticism of "solarism" by William E. Gladstone in the November issue. Müller denied that he was trying to give *all* mythology a solar origin.

17. Georgina Max Müller, *Life and Letters,* II, 381.

18. See Müller, *Selected Essays on Language, Mythology, and Religion* (London, 1881), I, 617-623, in "On the Philosophy of Mythology," and Blackie, *Horae Hellenicae: Essays and Discussions on some Important Points of Greek Philology and Antiquity* (London, 1874), pp. 167-196, "On the Scientific Interpretation of Popular Myths with special reference to Greek mythology."

19. Müller, *My Autobiography, A Fragment* (New York, 1909), pp. 147-150, and also *Contributions to the Science of Mythology,* I, 303.

20. Chs. 5 and 6 in *My Autobiography* give rich details on Müller's early years in France and England.

21. Müller, *Lectures on the Science of Language, delivered at the Royal Institution of Great Britain in February, March, April, and May, 1863,* 2nd Ser. (New York, 1869), p. 371, in the lecture on "Metaphor."

22. Müller, *Natural Religion: The Gifford Lectures Delivered before the University of Glasgow in 1888* (London, 1889), p. 487. For these squibs see "The Oxford Solar Myth" by the Rev. R. F. Littledale, in Max Müller, *Comparative Mythology, An Essay,* ed. Abram Smythe Palmer (London and New York, n. d.), pp. xxxi-xlvii, reprinted from *Kottabos,* a magazine of Trinity College, Dublin, No. 5 (1870), which proves Max Müller to be a solar hero; anon., "John Gilpin as a Solar Hero," *Fraser's Magazine,* n. s. XXIII (March, 1881), 353-371; E. B. Tylor, *Primitive Culture,* 3rd ed. (London, 1891), I, 319-320 (the Song of Sixpence, Cortès, and Julius Caesar are "solarized").

Although the Rev. A. Smythe Palmer reprinted a solar-myth satire along with Max Müller's essay, he himself belongs to the school of solar interpretation. His own "Introductory Preface on Solar Mythology," pp. v-xxix, while deploring the excesses of Cox, completely endorses and supports Müller's "epoch-making" treatise with a barrage of references, from ethnology and poetry, on the primal role of the sun in the mind of man. In his own work, Palmer carries out Müller's methods: *The Samson-Saga and its Place in Comparative Religion* (London, 1913), analyzes the solar character of Samson; *Folk-Etymology, A Dictionary of Verbal Corruptions or Words Perverted in Form or Meaning, by False Derivation or Mistaken Analogy* (London, 1882), and *The Folk and their Word-Lore* (London and New York, 1904) both illustrate what Müller called "modern mythology" or contemporary examples of the disease of language.

23. Müller, *India: What Can it Teach Us? A Course of Lectures delivered before the University of Cambridge* (New York, 1883), p. 216. Cf. these similar statements: "I look upon the sunrise and sunset, on the daily return of day and night, on the battle between light and darkness, on the whole solar drama in all its details that is acted every day, every month, every year, in heaven and in earth, as the principal subject of early mythology" (*Lectures on the Science of Language, Second Series,* p. 537). ". . . there was but one name by which they [mythopoeic men] could express love— there was but one similitude for the roseate bloom that betrays the dawn of love—it was the blush of the day, the rising of the sun. 'The sun has risen,' they said, where we say, 'I love'; 'The sun has

set,' they said, where we say, 'I have loved'" (*Chips from a German Workshop,* [New York, 1872], II, 128, from "Comparative Mythology," [1856]). "Was not the Sunrise to him [mythopoeic man] the first wonder, the first beginning of all reflection, all thought, all philosophy? Was it not to him the first revelation, the first beginning of all trust, of all religion?" (*Selected Essays on Language, Mythology, and Religion* [London, 1881], I, 599-600). "'Is everything the Dawn? Is everything the Sun?' This question I had asked myself many times before it was addressed to me by others . . . . but I am bound to say that my own researches lead me again and again to the dawn and the sun as the chief burden of the myths of the Aryan race" (*Lectures on the Science of Language, Second Series,* p. 520).

24. Müller, "Jupiter, the Supreme Aryan God," *Lectures on the Science of Language, Second Series,* pp. 432-480; "The Lesson of Jupiter," *Nineteenth Century,* XVIII (Oct., 1885), 626-650.

25. Müller himself distinguishes between the "solar" and the "meterological" theories of comparative mythology, the latter championed by Adalbert Kuhn (*Lectures on the Science of Language, Second Series,* pp. 538-540). He attempted to reconcile them by assigning a common root to the meanings of sun, lightning, and fire (*Physical Religion* [New York, 1891], p. 186). See Lang, "Myths and Mythologists," 52-53, for these disagreements; in *Modern Mythology,* p. 35, he gives a table of varying interpretations of Cronus, and makes the point that these differences were unknown to the English public, familiar only with Müller and not with continental mythologists (pp. 1-2).

26. E.g., *Natural Religion,* p. 449: ". . . no one who is not an expert, has anything to say here." In 1897 Müller wrote Lang personally, "Still less could I understand why you should have attacked me, or rather my masters, without learning Sanscrit. . . ." (*Life and Letters,* II, 381).

27. Müller, *Natural Religion,* p. 441; "Solar Myths," 904-905.

28. Müller, *Lectures on the Science of Languages, Second Series,* pp. 556-568, in Lecture XII, "Modern Mythology."

29. See especially "The Method of Folklore" and "The Myth of Cronus" in *Custom and Myth* (London, 1884, and later editions).

30. Lang, "Mythology," *Encyclopaedia Britannica,* 9th ed. (Chicago, 1895), XXII, 137-141, "The System of Max Müller."

31. Lang, "Myths and Mythologists," 56*n.*

32. Lang, *Myth, Ritual, and Religion* (London, New York, Bombay, and Calcutta, 1913), II, 193-194.

33. Lang, *Myth, Ritual, and Religion* (London, 1887), II, 196.

34. See, e.g., Müller's concluding remarks in his review of Cox's

A Manual of Mythology, in *Chips from a German Workshop,* II, 154-159, where he points out the possibility of ancient myths being transferred to historical heroes; and his expression of misgivings about "The Analogical School," in *Natural Religion,* p. 486.

35. Müller, "The Savage," *Nineteenth Century,* XVII (Jan., 1885), 109-132; *Contributions to the Science of Mythology,* I, 7, 185 et seq.; *Anthropological Religion,* Appendix III, "On Totems and Their Various Origin," pp. 403-410; *Lectures on the Origin and Growth of Religion as Illustrated by the Religions of India* (London, 1878), pp. 52-127.

36. Müller, *Anthropological Religion,* Appendix V, "On the Untrustworthiness of Anthropological Evidence," pp. 413-435.

37. Müller, *Contributions to the Science of Mythology,* I, 280.

38. Müller, *Contributions to the Science of Mythology,* I, 277, 290.

39. Müller, *Contributions to the Science of Mythology,* II, 600.

40. Müller, *Natural Religion,* p. 441.

41. Müller iterates the necessity to learn languages, and not simply engage in the "pleasant reading" of folklore, obsessively in *Contributions to the Science of Mythology,* I, 5, 23-24, 28, 128, 232, 286; II, 462, 830-831.

42. Müller, *Chips from a German Workshop,* II, "On Manners and Customs," 248-283, esp. 260.

43. Müller, *Contributions to the Science of Mythology,* I, 143; *Lectures on the Origin and Growth of Religion,* p. 91.

44. Müller, *Natural Religion,* p. 505.

45. Müller, *Natural Religion,* p. 515; *Life and Letters,* II, 129; *Anthropological Religion,* pp. 169-171, where Müller gives the fullest details of his contact with an educated Mohawk.

46. Müller, "The Savage," 117; *Natural Religion,* pp. 515-517; "Mythology among the Hottentots," *Nineteenth Century* (Jan., 1882), pp. 33-38. For Müller's correspondence with Horatio Hale, president of the American Folklore Society, see *Life and Letters,* II, 117-118, 129, 145-146. Thus he writes in 1883, "I am glad to hear of your projects. I feel sure that there is no time to be lost in securing the floating fragments of the great shipwreck of the American languages. When you have stirred up a national interest in it for the North of America, you should try to form a Committee for the South. The Emperor of Brazil would be sure to help, provided the work is done by *real scholars*" (145-146).

47. Müller, *Lectures on the Origin and Growth of Religion,* pp. 74-75.

48. William Wyatt Gill, *Myths and Songs from the South Pacific*

(London, 1876). In his preface (pp. v-xviii) Müller explicitly rejects any one explanation for mythology, whether fetishism or the disease of language.

49. Müller, *Contributions to the Science of Mythology*, I, 11.

50. Müller, "The Savage," p. 111.

51. Müller, *Anthropological Religion,* pp. 173-180, "The Andaman Islanders."

52. Müller, "Solar Myths," pp. 900-922, esp. 902, 906, 919.

53. Müller, *Natural Religion,* p. 516; *India: What Can It Teach Us?,* pp. 169-175.

54. Müller, *Anthropological Religion,* Appendix VIII, "The Kalevala," pp. 440-446.

55. Müller, *Selected Essays on Language, Mythology and Religion,* I, 609-615, in ch. X, "On the Philosophy of Mythology." Note, e.g., "Among Finns and Lapps, among Zulus and Maoris, among Khonds and Karens, we sometimes find the most startling analogies. . . ." (p. 615).

56. Müller, *Physical Religion,* pp. 286-293, in Lecture XII, "Religion, Myth, and Custom."

57. Müller, *Chips from a German Workshop,* V (New York, 1881), p. 89; "How much the student of Aryan mythology and ethnology may gain for his own progress by allowing himself a wider survey over the traditions and customs of the whole human race, is best known to those who have studied the works of Klemm, Waitz, Bastian, Sir John Lubbock, Mr. Tylor, and Dr. Callaway" (in "On the Philosophy of Mythology," 1871).

58. Lang's comments in *Modern Mythology,* p. xx, alleging prejudice on Müller's part against ethnological collections, are manifestly unfair. The unbiased reader will, I believe, agree with the statements of Müller that he was not an adversary but more nearly a collaborator with Lang (*Contributions to the Science of Mythology,* I, 11; *Life and Letters,* II, 381, where Müller writes Lang, ". . . I am perfectly certain that some good may be got from the study of savages for the elucidation of Aryan myths. I never could find out why I should be thought to be opposed to Agriology, because I was an aryologist. *L'un n'empeche pas l'autre,*" 8 July 1897). Note that Müller, as well as Lang, was a charter member of the Folk-Lore Society in 1878.

59. Müller, "Solar Myths," p. 916.

60. Müller, *Natural Religion,* pp. 508-510, and 511*n*.

61. Müller, *Contributions to the Science of Mythology,* I, 235 et seq.; II, 433-435.

62. Lang, *Modern Mythology,* pp. 85, 142-143. Lang writes that he begged Müller not to read the book, and vowed not to criticize

his ideas again ("Max Müller," *Contemporary Review,* LXXVIII [1900], 785).

63. *Folk-Lore,* X (1899), 346-348. Hartland was then engaged in a dispute with Lang over the nature of Australian aboriginal religious ideas.

64. See Lang's Preface to the new edition of *Myth, Ritual, and Religion,* 2 vols. (London, New York, Bombay, and Calcutta, 1913), I, xvi.

65. Lang, *Myth, Ritual, and Religion,* 1913 ed., II, 298, 105; cf. 1887 ed., II, 280, 81.

66. These are combined in No. 721 of Everyman's Library, *Tales of Ancient Greece* (London and New York, 1915, frequently reprinted), whose introduction has no doubt misled countless younger readers into interpreting all Greek myths as activities of the sun.

67. Cox, *The Mythology of the Aryan Nations,* 2 vols. (London, 1870, reprinted 1882), I, v-vii.

68. Cox, *The Mythology of the Aryan Nations,* I, 21n, 65n; II, 75-76.

69. Cox, *The Mythology of the Aryan Nations,* I, 168; cf. 49, 153, 291, 308, and *A Manual of Mythology in the Form of Question and Answer,* 1st American ed., from the 2nd London ed. (New York, 1868), pp. 39, 70, 78, 81, 104, 109, 117, 119, 211, for references to parallels between solar heroes; indeed, Cox never introduces a hero without indicating these parallels.

70. Cox, *The Mythology of the Aryan Nations,* I, 267.

71. Cox, *The Mythology of the Aryan Nations,* I, 170n, 308, 322-325, 409, 135n.

72. Cox, *An Introduction to the Science of Comparative Mythology and Folklore* (London, 1881), pp. 309, 307.

73. Cox, *The Mythology of the Aryan Nations,* I, 159n, 132n. Frequently the fairy-tale hero wears a "garment of humiliation" representative of the toiling, unrequited sun.

74. Cox, *The Mythology of the Aryan Nations,* I, 247n.

75. Müller, *Natural Religion,* p. 495.

76. Cox, *The Mythology of the Aryan Nations,* I, 113.

77. "The Master Thief" is Type 1525 in Antti Aarne and Stith Thompson, *The Types of the Folk-Tale* (Helsinki, 1928); "Rhampsinitus" is Type 950. Cox used this supposed tale for evidence against borrowing; see his "The Migration of Popular Stories," *Fraser's Magazine,* n.s. XXII (July, 1880), 96-111.

78. Cox, *The Mythology of the Aryan Nations,* I, 145.

79. Cox, *An Introduction to the Science of Comparative Mythology and Folklore,* p. 7n.

80. Lang, "Household Tales: Their Origin, Diffusion, and Relation to the Higher Myths," Introduction to *Grimm's Household Tales*, with the author's notes, trans. and ed. Margaret Hunt, 2 vols. (London, 1910), I, xxiv-xxv, xxxv, xl.

81. See Lang's note, "Household Tales: Their Origin, Diffusion, and Relation to the Higher Myths," p. xxiv: "When *The Mythology of the Aryan Nations* was written, philologists were inclined to believe that their analysis of language was the true, perhaps the only key, to knowledge of what men had been in the pre-historic past. It is now gnerally recognized . . . that the sciences of Anthropology and Archaeology also throw much light on the human past. . . ."

82. Robert Brown, *The Great Dionysiak Myth*, 2 vols. (London, 1877-1878), I, 162.

83. Brown, *The Great Dionysiak Myth*, I, vi; II, 334.

84. Other relevant publications are *The Religion of Zoroaster* (1879), *The Religion and Mythology of the Aryans of Northern Europe* (1880), *Language, and Theories of its Origin* (1881), *The Law of Kosmic Order* (1882), *Eridanus, River and Constellation* (1883), *Researches into the Origin of the Primitive Constellations of the Greeks, Phoenicians, and Babylonians* (1899, 1900), *Mr. Gladstone As I Knew Him, And Other Essays* (1902), esp. "Studies in Pausanias," pp. 93-235.

85. Brown, *The Great Dionysiak Myth*, I, 4; "Reply to Prof. Max Müller on 'The Etymology of Dionysos,'" *Academy*, (19 Aug. 1882), cited in Brown, *The Myth of Kirkê: including the visit of Odysseus to the Shades. An Homerik Study* (London, 1883), p. 83n.

86. E.g., Brown, *The Great Dionysiak Myth*, II, 139-140, [Theseus and the Minotaur], I, 420-426 [statue of Demeter]; "Posidônic Theory of Rev. G. W. Cox," *Poseidôn: A Link Between Semite, Hamite, and Aryan* (London, 1872), pp. 5-9. In his preface to a new edition of *The Mythology of the Aryan Nations* (1882), Cox pays especial tribute to the researches of Robert Brown. In *The Unicorn: A Mythological Investigation* (London, 1881), p. 73, Brown cites the acceptance of his view of Bakchos-Melqarth by Cox.

87. Brown, *The Great Dionysiak Myth*, II, 140, 213; *Semitic Influence in Hellenic Mythology, with special reference to the recent mythological works of the Rt. Hon. Prof. F. Max Müller and Mr. Andrew Lang* (London, Edinburgh, Oxford, 1898), p. 202.

88. Brown, *The Myth of Kirkê*, pp. 163, 92.

89. Brown, *The Great Dionysiak Myth*, I, 229, ". . . one key will never open all locks"; *Poseidôn*, pp. 79-80.

90. Brown, *Poseidôn,* pp. 39-40; *The Great Dionysiak Myth,* I, 229.

91. Brown, *The Myth of Kirkê,* pp. 157-162.

92. Brown, *The Great Dionysiak Myth,* II, 9-11; also *The Unicorn,* pp. 73-78, "The Contest between the Lion and the Leopard." In *The Myth of Kirkê,* Brown resolves two variants of the death of Odysseus as the same solar myth, by making a ray-fish the young sun that drops on the bald head of Odysseus, the old sun (p. 23).

93. Brown, *The Unicorn,* p. 1; *The Myth of Kirkê,* pp. 47, 53.

94. Brown, *The Great Dionysiak Myth,* II, 332.

95. Brown, *Poseidôn,* pp. 2, 110-116.

96. Brown, *The Myth of Kirkê,* pp. 167, 101.

97. Brown, *Semitic Influence in Hellenic Mythology,* p. ix.

98. Brown, *Semitic Influence in Hellenic Mythology,* pp. 23-24; cf. Müller, *Contributions to the Science of Comparative Mythology,* I, vii.

99. Brown, *Semitic Influence in Hellenic Mythology,* pp. 29-31, 54-66.

100. Brown, *Semitic Influence in Hellenic Mythology,* pp. 205-215.

101. Brown, *Semitic Influence in Hellenic Mythology,* pp. 30-31, 34, 150.

102. Lang, *Custom and Myth* (London, 1893), p. 137.

103. Lang, "Moly and Mandragora," in *Custom and Myth,* p. 155*n.*

104. This polemical preface appears only in the 1898 ed., and was withdrawn in later reprintings of *Custom and Myth.* It is titled "Apollo, the Mouse, and Mr. Robert Brown, Junior, F.S.A., M.R.S.A.," and occupies pp. i-xix.

105. Gubernatis, *Zoological Mythology, or The Legends of Animals,* 2 vols. (New York and London, 1872), II, p. 425. Gubernatis also compiled a mythological herbarium, *La Mythologie des Plantes, ou Les Légendes du Règne Végétal,* 2 vols. (Paris, 1878), in dictionary form; the first volume treats mythical heroes and phenomena with plant associations (the sun is like a tree), the second considers plants as they appear in myths. Gubernatis diverges from Müller on "Bernacles," which he traces to a bird-producing tree in India (I, 65-70).

106. Gubernatis, *Zoological Mythology,* I, 370; II, 337, 322, 356, 181, 390.

107. Gubernatis, *Zoological Mythology,* I, 244. Cf. this interpretation with that of the modern psychoanalytical school, which considers "beans" and "stalk" as symbols for the testicles and

penis, and sees the tale as a masturbation fantasy (William H. Desmonde, "Jack and the Beanstalk," *American Imago,* VIII [Sept. 1951], 287-288).

108. Gubernatis, *Zoological Mythology,* II, 113. This is Type 38, "Claw in Split Tree."

109. Gubernatis, *Zoological Mythology,* I, 258*n.* Motif B251.1.2.2., "Cows speak to one another on Christmas" (Stith Thompson, *Motif-Index of Folk-Literature* [Bloomington, Ind., 1932-36]), is well-known, but the death prophecy is not. I heard the full tale from a Mississippi-born Negro.

110. Brown, *The Myth of Kirkê,* pp. 54-55.

111. Lang, *Custom and Myth,* p. 117.

112. Unsigned review, *The Scotsman,* 26 Dec. 1872. The lengthy review omits to mention the phallic as well as solar interpretations rendered by Gubernatis (see, e.g., *Zoological Mythology,* II, 9-10), with far more boldness than by squeamish Robert Brown (*The Myth of Kirkê,* p. 23*n; The Great Dionysiak Myth,* I, 7*n*).

113. Daniel Brinton, *The Myths of the New World: A Treatise on the Symbolism and Mythology of the Red Race of America,* 3rd ed., revised (Philadelphia, 1896), p. 109. In spite of its viewpoint, this edition is very favorably reviewed in *Folk-Lore,* VIII (1897), 57-59 (unsigned), alongside an equally favorable review of Franz Boas, *Indianische Sagen von der nord-pacifischen Küste Amerikas* (pp. 59-62), the study which upset Brinton's anti-diffusionism. See Robert H. Lowie, *The History of Ethnological Theory* (New York, 1937), p. 146.

114. Brinton, *The Myths of the New World,* pp. 194-199.

115. Brinton, *The Myths of the New World,* pp. 206, 94 et seq., 252, 163, 168.

116. Müllers, "Solar Myths," p. 909.

117. Brinton, *The Myths of the New World,* p. 198, quoting from Müller, *The Science of Language, Second Series.* Brinton refers to both Müller and Cox in his introduction to *American Hero-Myths: A Study in the Native Religions of the Western Continent* (Philadelphia, 1882), pp. 23, 31*n.*

118. Brinton, *The Myths of the New World,* pp. 134, 139.

119. Müller, "Solar Myths," p. 911; also *Natural Religion,* pp. 512-513.

120. Lang, "Myths and Mythologists," p. 64; also *Myth, Ritual and Religion* (London, 1887), II, 57-59.

121. Lang, "Myths and Mythologists," p. 64. Brinton criticized Lang for degrading the savage spiritually—the position Lang later

recanted—in *Essays of an Americanist* (Philadelphia, 1890), p. 102.

122. John Fiske, *Myths and Myth-Makers: Old Tales and Superstitions interpreted by Comparative Mythology,* 11th ed. (Boston and New York, 1888), ch. 2, "The Descent of Fire," pp. 37-68; and Lang, *Custom and Myth,* "The Divining Rod," pp. 180-196.

123. Fiske, *Myths and Myth-Makers,* p. 123. Cf. Müller, *Physical Religion,* pp. 186-187, "Reconciliation of the Solar and Meteoric Theories."

124. Fiske, *Myths and Myth-Makers,* pp. 195-196n.

125. Fiske, *Myths and Myth-Makers,* pp. 211, 192-194, 204n.

126. Fiske, *Myths and Myth-Makers,* pp. 151, 144-148, 238.

127. Sidney Hartland, *Mythology and Folktales: Their Relation and Interpretation,* 2nd ed. (London, 1914), p. 13.

128. In a gracious letter to Mrs. Max Müller after her husband's death Lang wrote, "Our little systems have their day, or their hour: as knowledge advances they pass into the history of the efforts of pioneers" (Georgina Max Müller, *Life and Letters,* II, 452).

MYTH, METAPHOR, AND SIMILE

BY REIDAR TH. CHRISTIANSEN

O NE is inclined to use such terms as "myth" and "mythical" with a certain diffidence, and the reason is that these terms, in general usage, have been extended and have come to denote two different things. For example, a distinction is usually drawn between "historical" and "mythical" legends, and the latter group, by far the most popular and most richly varied, is, in a more general way, taken to include stories in which the intervention of non-human forces and powers is the main point. At the same time, however, "myth" carries another set of associations; according to the definition generally given, it embodies "legends of cosmogony and of gods and heroes," to quote the formula given by the *Encyclopaedia Britannica*. Current traditional legends only very rarely relate anything about the gods and their doings, but there are any number of stories in which beings—non-human, but close neighbors of man—constantly interfere in human activities and, therefore, command respectful attention. These beings belong decidedly to this world, and none ever attained, in the stories and conceptions of those who believed in them, the status of a god. Yet they are constantly referred to as "mythical" beings, and the reason may be that, as the belief in them waned, they were excluded from everyday life and relegated to the vague and frightening zone where everything that was an object of religious belief was assumed to belong. The ghosts, on the other hand, were decidedly still of this world because they to a large extent still figure in the belief and in the experience of man.

As for mythology, the distinction made between a "lower" and a "higher" mythology seems to be of primary importance, even if the former should rather be called "folk belief" or, to be more exact, "ancient folk belief." In this way one would stress the fundamental continuity between folk beliefs of the changing periods. The exact relationship between the two strata of mythology is difficult to define, but the "higher," with its rich and colorful store of tales, whether of the gods of the classics or of the sterner, less gracious deities of the Norse, has a different—it might be said a more sophisticated —character, than has oral tradition and belief. We might question whether people ever did actually believe in these gods, or, if they believed in the gods themselves, whether they believed in the tales told about them. Perhaps an analogy might be the relationship between general religious belief of the present day and theology, for at least both theology and mythology have the function of giving an explanation of those fundamental problems that confront, and have ever confronted, mankind. So had also traditional legend and belief,[1] but their answer was much simpler and more evident, whether given in story or in action.

As a consequence, a connection between the "higher" mythology and later folk tradition is hard to find, and traditional legend has few, if any, additions to make to our knowledge of the ancient gods.[2] But the conservative tenacity of oral tradition offers a direct connection with "lower" mythology, i.e., the background to all these elaborate tales about the doings of the gods, or of the "heroes," to return to the definition quoted above, which has evidently been altered to include the "demigods" of ancient fame.

Parallels between myths and epic oral tradition certainly exist, but can such similarities only be explained by assuming the myth to be the original source? In most cases, and probably in all, the fact seems to be that both myth and legend took such motifs and incidents from the same source —from oral tradition.

Legends and folktales are, however, only one branch of oral tradition after all, and reminiscences of myth and of the ancient gods may equally well have survived in the names of places and persons, in a saying, in a rhyme or a turn of speech, and, to come to the subject of the present paper, in a metaphor or a simile. The latter occur especially in the traditional riddles, and our intention is to examine somewhat more closely a few specimens of riddles for objects that were also acknowledged subjects for a myth. Within the narrow frame of a riddle a complete story could hardly be condensed, and even a metaphor referring to some special definite myth seems, to say the least, extremely rare. The possible connection between mythology and the metaphors of riddles has, therefore, been sought in a more general way, assuming that both represented some special "mythical way of thinking." Such ideas were first formulated by German scholars: Christian G. Heyne, F. Strauss, later by W. Schwartz, and, to a certain degree, further developed by W. Mannhardt.[3] Stressing the illogical and irrational character of many elements in folklore, such elements were called "mythical," and were deduced from certain aspects of human psychology, from processes akin to those from which have sprung the imagery of poetry and poetic diction. However, while a poet could consciously direct his flow of associations, primitive man was assumed to ignore the distance between his direct impression of facts and the expressions he found for them. His expressions, his images, were to him actual realities, and the connection between fact and image was to him, it was maintained, so real that image or symbol was equated with the object itself. In such a state of mind were hidden the "roots of poetry" as well as the ultimate roots of metaphors and motifs embedded in traditional matter.

Such sweeping, systematic constructions have in later periods met with criticism and reservations, probably mainly because such conceptions of the active, creative fancy in the minds of man at an early stage in his development do not seem to be compatible with the evidence of the vast mass of ethnographical information made accessible within the last decades. Probably nobody will deny that such things as metaphors and similes were used, and still are used, by the "primitive" mind (the term being used in a vague general sense, and with the reservation that the nature of a really primitive mind is, and ever will be, unknown). It seemed necessary to repeat this often expressed qualification in view of the mass of evidence quoted in support of and as illustration of so many widesweeping theories. What does no longer seem to be tenable is the idea that at any time man, illogically or "prelogically," did actually *believe* in the identity of an object and the metaphor he used to denote it. On the contrary, an accurate and intimate knowledge of his surroundings and the possibilities they offered was a main condition for his maintaining his precarious existence, or to quote a German writer: "Die enge, keine Illusion zulassende Vertrautheit mit seiner Umgebung ist eines der wesentlichen Mittel des tiefstehenden Nomaden den Kampf ums Dasein bestechen zu können."[4]

The disinterested intellectual function of the mind of primitive man was, by such general theories, given a part far too prominent, and was even carried to the length that the myths proper, i.e., the legends about gods and heroes, originally arose from the misunderstanding of a metaphor: witness the catch-phrase that myths were nothing else than the result of "a disease of language." Such conceptions have by now been rejected and discredited by most students, and other explanations of the origin of symbol, simile, and metaphor, which stress the practical or the emotional factors in their development, have been offered. Their function may have been to supply the means of comprehending and making familiar new phenomena that had to be mastered, and more especially, the metaphor has been connected with the world-wide practice of using substitute words—"tabu words" —to avoid the supposed danger involved in referring to certain things too directly by using their common names.[5] This curious practice is, as already stated, followed in many parts of the world, both by races that may in a certain sense be referred to as primitive and by several European races, and seems on the whole to be connected with activities that involve a certain amount of risk, as, e.g., fishing and hunting. The explanation is, therefore, probably to be sought in ethnological factors. Such words have been exhaustively studied, and they are hardly metaphors. In most cases, they are mere artificial circumscriptions not otherwise in use.

Whether, then, at some very early stage man started using metaphors and similes just to familiarize himself with new things, or just to avoid arousing imagined dangers by mentioning by name potential carriers of such, this strange, evasive playing with words had a function in his life. Accordingly, the possible connection between myth and metaphor acquires a new aspect. To such questions as that of the origin of metaphors, or the origin of speech and music, etc., only an answer of a highly speculative kind can be given, but the question itself has little importance in explaining the metaphors found in oral tradition, especially in riddles where they naturally are an important element. Even if they, at the outset, may have meant the solution of some actual problem, they soon became the recognized property of poets, and this applies not only to the more complex metaphors used by an individual poet, intent upon following associations of his own, but also to the infinitely simpler metaphors to be found in the traditional riddle. The difference between these two types can be summed up by the word, "traditional." The original conception, by becoming the property of many, immediately became subject to the laws, perhaps better called tendencies, which determine the development of traditional matter. In their migrations, and even such minor items as riddles travel with surprising ease from country to country, they attained a less individual type and became acceptable to all. Their migrations were facilitated by their pointed brevity and even more by rhyme, qualities that at the same time were, to a certain extent, a guarantee against too sweeping alterations. Essentially, however, the metaphors coined by an individual poet and those familiar to all in a riddle are of the same type, and neither had its origin in even the reminiscence of a myth.

Myths and mythology, even while using motifs and incidents equally ubiquitous, still have a decidedly local character, while riddles, in which as a matter of course the influence of local environment, natural and social, is also easily felt—there are, in fact, riddles where no solution is possible without an intimate familiarity with local life—may pass with ease from country to country and be accepted by a new audience, provided that both the idea and the metaphor have a common appeal concerned with things familiar to everybody. Hence the difficulty of tracing any one of these riddles back to its ultimate origin.

As an illustration of the relationship between myth and metaphor it seemed natural to select for some brief notes those riddles that referred to objects which were likewise fit subjects for a myth, i.e., natural phenomena, such as sun, moon, rain, etc. In the tradition of Scandinavian countries the riddle for the rainbow offers a good instance, as it has, according to the explanation given in ancient literature, distinct mythological associations. According to Snorre, the historian, the gods built a bridge to join heaven to earth. He refers to the bridge in his compendium, compiled to teach the poets the difficult art of introducing more or less intricate allusions to the gods. One part of his book, a prose account of the gods, is the main source for our knowledge of Norse mythology. It is written in the form of a dialogue between someone called "the Wanderer" and the "Three High Ones," probably on the pattern of Christian conceptions. He writes: "Then said the Wanderer: 'Where is the road from earth to heaven?' The High-one answered, slightly smiling: 'That is no wise question. Have you never been told that the gods built a bridge to heaven from earth, and its name is Bifróst, and you are sure to have seen it, but maybe you will call it the rainbow. It has three colours, is built with cunning craft and is exceedingly strong, and yet it will be broken at the end of the world.'"[6]

Whatever foundation Snorre had in ancient belief, his explanation of the rainbow as a bridge corresponds to a metaphor used in a group of rainbow riddles. It is to be expected that a phenomenon as spectacular and as evanescent as the rainbow should be a fit subject for a riddle, and in the tradition of the Scandinavian countries several types of these are found. The one most popular does not, however, use a metaphor at all. It consists of three or four descriptive lines, rounded off with a mock promise to the one who has the solution. The following, for example, was recorded somewhere in Western Norway about the year 1850: *Høgt, høgt krokutt bøygt/og underleg skapt./Kan du taka gåta mi fatt/ ska du få sove hjå meg i natt* 'High, high/Crooked and bent/And curiously shaped/If you catch the meaning of my riddle/You may sleep with me tonight.' The riddle was recorded from many Norwegian districts, and the variants differ only on some minor points. Thus the first line, obviously too short in the version quoted, is as a rule rounded off in some way or other, and another line pointing out the many colors may be added. Most of the epithets used are modifications, real or artificial, of the words "high and bent."

The riddle, in practically the same words, is also very popular in Denmark and Sweden, and as it is also widely known in Northern Germany, there is some reason to conclude that at some time and in some way, it was carried from the Continent towards the North.[7]

Other types of rainbow riddles use a metaphor. Among these are some that call it a bridge, just as it was, according to Snorre, said to the wanderer. A version from Central Norway (Telemark) may be quoted as a specimen: *Der gjeng ei bru ivi ei å/ enkje æ ho roti/ å enkje æ ho rå / enkje æ ho hogganes, ganganes på* 'There is a bridge across a river/ Neither is it rotten nor is it raw/ No one can walk across it/ And nobody cut bits from it.' To judge from the number recorded this type of riddle is decidedly less popular than the first one, but still variants exist from most parts of the country, and recur further South, in Denmark as in Sweden. Variations are also few and unimportant in this case. However, once a tree was substituted for the bridge; perhaps this was borrowed from other riddles, or suggested by the statement that no one might cut a chip from the bridge.[8]

These two types seem to be those most widely known, but several others have been recorded. Most of them seem to have parallels elsewhere. It seems natural that the colors of the rainbow should be stressed by the riddle, but few Norwegian variants mention them. One is: "What is that? A towel sewn with silk. No one ever took it into his hands." And, with a reference to the shape: "A golden belt is hanging in

the wood. All may look at it; no one touch it."[9] This type is
known elsewhere and, choosing a couple of variants at random, the similarity is striking. One is: "In the field a piece of
silk in five colors. Neither you nor I can grasp it." Another:
"On the sky there hangs a kerchief in red colors, so it is said."
Such close parallels might seem to involve a definite connection between the variants, but in this particular case any
connection seems to be impossible; one of these riddles comes
from the Yakut, the other from the Mongols—both very far
from Norway. They are quoted from Taylor's extremely interesting collection of Mongol riddles.[10] Such a case serves as
an excellent illustration of how comparatively simple similes
have occurred to people even in widely different environ-
ments. In this case the same metaphor was used independently in places far apart; in other cases there may be a certain pattern that is popular and may emerge anywhere. Thus
in Northern Norway the following rainbow riddle was recorded: "There was a man, but there was no man. He walked
on a road, but there was no road. Can you guess what man
that was?"[11] As shown by Taylor, the pattern of assertions
and denial has a long pedigree; it can be applied to almost any
subject and offers a correspondingly wide choice of solutions.

Of these riddles only the one in which the rainbow was
called a bridge could with some reason have a connection
with the bridge of the gods, the Bifróst. According to Moltke
Moe there was no "conscious, spontaneous selection of the
metaphor" either with Snorre or with the makers of the
riddle, and the proof for this assertion he found in the "obviously irrational character of the equation, rainbow—
bridge."[12] However, such reasoning does not sound convincing. Any number of equally "irrational" comparisons and
metaphors could be pointed out, both from individual poetry
and from tradition. Often the very startling and unexpected
quality of a metaphor used was a means to stress a certain
point and to let loose the flow of associations one meant to
raise. In this case the constellation, bridge—rainbow, did not
seem irrational or far-fetched at all; it is, in fact, so common
that an attempt to trace it to some original source seems an
incongruous task.

It may be well worth noticing that according to Snorre the

rainbow—bridge joined heaven and earth, while in the riddle the bridge spanned a river, and probably all would admit that in this function the simile is more natural. This may be the reason why elsewhere in Norwegian tradition, as, e.g., in the ancient visionary poem, the *Draumkvœde,* and in the small lyrical quatrains, the *stev,* the bridge to heaven is not the Bifróst rainbow, but is associated with the Gjallarbru, which, according to Snorre and other sources, spanned the river between the world of man and that of the dead.[13] This bridge the visionary passed "with grave-mould in his mouth" just as did the deceased, and the bridge itself "spanned the high heavens and was swept by the winds." This bridge seems to have some connection with ancient mythical ideas, at least with regard to its name.

The rainbow—bridge is a concept widely known on the Continent, and is not of Norwegian origin at all. As a single instance of the idea, a traditional German poem may be quoted: *Wenn der jüngste Tag wird werden, / Fallen die Sternlein auf die Erden, / Beugen sich die Bäumelein, / singen die lieben Engelein. / Kommt der liebe Gott gezogen / Auf einem schönen Regenbogen.*[14] Further instances may be found in many quarters, e.g., refer to the Iris of the classics.[15]

This is the rainbow—bridge in a special function, offering an open road to heaven; but apart from that, the equation, rainbow to bridge, has occurred to people in various parts of the world. As for riddles for the rainbow, they, according to Taylor, "vary greatly among themselves, and few, if any resemble the English texts."[16] The riddles quoted by Taylor refer to the colors of the rainbow (Nos. 654 and 655), adding that it is high up in the air (No. 1284). Of chronological interest is a riddle (No. 1570), which contains a reference to Cromwell. Strangely enough this riddle was recorded in exactly the same words from Illinois.[17]

To individual poets the bridge also suggested itself naturally. Schiller wrote a poem about the rainbow, the first verse of which is as follows: *Von Perlen baut sich eine Brücke / Hoch über einen grauen See. / Sie baut, sich auf im Augenblicke, / Und schwindelnd steigt sie in die Höh.*[18] There are two more verses describing other strange aspects of this bridge: ships pass easily under it, it cannot carry any load, and it dissolves as one gets near it. Schiller called his poem a riddle; he may have developed some traditional idea, but such an explanation hardly seems necessary. The idea seems so natural that it would as easily suggest itself to poets as to the makers of riddles anywhere. The ultimate origin of a metaphor like this is of course impossible to ascertain; it seems natural to look for it neither in myth nor in folk belief, but in the creative, active imagination of man, naturally associating the one with the other. One may also add that such an idea would hardly occur to anybody if the bridge did not have an arch, this point being the essence of the comparison— a fact that further seems to hint that the metaphor was not created before such bridges became known, and hardly in a primitive community.

Even primitive people could not have failed to notice and speculate upon the rainbow,[19] and among such races stories are occasionally told about it that, with some justification, might be called myths. Spencer and Gillen relate that the Kaitish tribes of Central Australia believe that the rainbow is the son of the rain and with filial care is always anxious to prevent his father from falling down. When it appears at a time when rain is wanted, they sing or enchant it away. "This story seems to contain the essentials of a myth, a rite, and a story told to explain it. Of another tribe it is said that they tremble at the sight of the rainbow, because they think it is a net spread, by some powerful spirit, to catch their shadows."[20]

Riddles of the rainbow seem to be far less numerous than riddles for other celestial phenomena, such as thunder, sun, moon, and stars. They have, however, a special interest to the problem of the relationship between myth and metaphor, because both by riddle and myth the rainbow was said to be a bridge, if Snorre really had any ancient authority for his statement. A detailed study of all similar metaphors would far exceed the limit of a paper. However, some notes on riddles of the sun are added because, in this particular case, the distance from the grandiose imagery used by the myths to the homely similes of the riddles is striking. Sun, moon, and stars are often given as the solution of a riddle, and similar metaphors may naturally be used for them all. According to the Greek, Helios drove the golden chariot of the sun across the firmament, and the splendor of the conception in comparison with scientific fact provoked Schiller to lament: *Da wo jetzt, wie unsere Weisen sagen / Seelenlos ein Feuerball sich dreht. / Lenkte damals seinen Feuerwagen / Helios in stiller Majestät.* In Norse mythology the course of the sun was, according to Snorre, explained in a similar way. He first gave an elaborate pedigree for the woman, Nótt (Night), and her son, Dag (Day). Night was of giant descent, dark and dreary, while Dag had a god as father, and was fair and bright. The Father-of-All took Night and Day up to his heaven and gave them each a horse and a chariot, in order that they should make the journey around the world in a day and night. Night goes first with a horse called Hrimfaxe, and the dew in the fields in the morning is flakes shaken from the bridle. The horse of Day is called Skinfaxe, and both earth and sky are lit by the splendor of its mane.[21]

Compared to this interpretation the metaphors found in riddles are homely and simple. Taylor, in a very interesting paper on poetry and riddles, stressed the homely character of the riddles, closely bound to man's immediate surroundings, and to familiar objects in the choice of similes.[22] There is no trace of the golden chariot, and in the traditional riddles of the Northern countries often no metaphor is used at all; instead they consist of a few descriptive lines referring to the most obvious aspects to the course of the sun or its light and heat, effects felt by everybody yet intangible to all. Accordingly, in many cases, not the sun itself, but sunshine, the sun rays, etc., would be the most correct solution, and it is often the one given. Some Norwegian specimens may be quoted, e.g., some referring to its daily course. A very common one is this: "What is it that walks over hills and valleys, over water and sea, through hay and straw, never making the slightest noise?" And stressing another characteristic: "It walks round the house, and cannot even be heard," or "It passes through the windows, even when they are shut." Such types are extremely simple, and may have other solutions as well, while others, referring to sunshine or the heat of the sun, usually also include some metaphor such as "gold lies over all the fields, yet no one can touch it." Similar but more picturesque is a riddle from the Faroe Isles: "It lies in the bog and never rots, it slides down the mountains and never breaks." Numerous parallels to such riddles are to be recorded from the other Northern countries, as well as from Irish and Gaelic-Scotch tradition.[23]

Such metaphors for sun rays and sunshine seem quite natural and obvious, while others may seem strange and the associations from which they came less obvious. This is the case when the sun itself is said to be a tree, a simile that on first sight seems rather incongruous. More easily comprehensible is a comparison of the rays of the sun to the branches of a tree, or to a golden stick, and when the solution offered is the sunset, especially into the sea, the simile of a vast golden tree is suggested; then the image is striking and the association intelligible. As an example one may quote a riddle from Sweden: "Who is standing in the sea churning with a stick of gold?" The riddle has also been recorded in Denmark, and, as a counterpart, there is a version from Norway, in which the solution is said to be the sun setting: "A tree is growing on the steep hillside, drooping over the sea, wholly covered with a coat of gold." In this case the simile seems quite natural, and the idea that the sun itself is called a tree may have come from some such association.[24]

The metaphor was obviously not immediately evident, and perhaps that is the reason why a theory was developed according to which the sun—tree had its origin in ancient mythological conceptions. In Norse legends stories were current of the great tree, Yggdrasil, a huge tree in the center of the universe, of which Snorre gave a detailed account in his compendium. A German mythologist, W. Schwartz, interpreted the tree as the sun, and explained in detail the whole series of wonders connected with it.[25] Some of his interpretations are extremely fantastic. Later the Norwegian scholar, S. Bugge, wrote that, although he would like to admit that there might be some possible connection between this tree of the world and the sun—tree of the riddles, there was no definite proof. Bugge quoted some Norwegian variants,[26] and Taylor added many more,[27] showing that this metaphor for the sun was current in riddles in many countries. A plausible explanation is that the solution was meant to be the rays of the sun or the sunset and, as suggested by Taylor, the very common riddle for the year may have been transferred to the sun. At the same time, however, such a simple explanation may not seem quite satisfactory because there may still be some ultimate connection between the sun—tree and a widely known concept of the world—tree, the Tree of Life. This is not the one of the Old Testament story, but rather the idea of a tree being the central pillar of the universe, a concept found not only in Europe but in other parts of the world as well.

Other smaller groups of riddles for sun and moon may deserve a cursory glance, i.e., those comparing these celestial bodies to an animal or to a thing. Taylor remarks that riddles "not unfrequently compare the sun to an animal," and quotes as an example the strange simile of the sun being a deer that no huntsman can hit (Nos. 391 and 392). In Scandinavian tradition such metaphors seem to be rare. The sun may be called a bird: "What kind of bird is that which every morning flies the same way and never returns?"[28] The point of association is the course of the sun. As a second line one would perhaps rather expect: "And comes back every morning anew;" this, however, might make the solution too easy. Better known are riddles in which the sun is said to be a horse or a cow. One may compare a Swedish instance: "A white mare on the shore, and its bridle gleaming."[29] In Irish and Scotch Gaelic riddles this metaphor is common, e.g., in one from the Hebrides: "A white mare on the hill with its head against the village," or one for sun and moon: "Two yellow cows on the Hill of the Winds, one during day and one during night."[30] The impression likely started from seeing the rising, or perhaps rather the setting, sun over the side of a hill. That such was the origin of the simile may seem even more likely as the cows are often said to be bald—having no horns. In a Norwegian riddle something of the same kind is found: "An ox is standing on a hill and is looking out over the sea. The buttons [i.e., on its horns] are of pure gold. You will not guess it today."[31]

With the same group one may also class a few divergent riddles, e.g., those in which the sun is represented as a living being. A Swedish specimen is rather striking, though very simple: "A large yellow head is rolling across a giant bridge. No one in our country can stop this head from rolling." More definite, but less striking, is this: "A huge body, but does not leave a shadow. Blind itself, it destroys the eye that looks at it too hard; at the same time it gives light to everybody."[32] More conventional and more pretty is another one: "A virgin is standing on a steep hill, casting light over the sea. She has such a number of buttons that you could not count them today." When in Norwegian folktales the trolls are tricked into looking at the sun, the traditional way of making them do so is to shout at them: "Look at the beautiful virgin coming," and the particular riddle may have borrowed the metaphor from folktale. The same riddle is recorded in the Faroe Isles.[33]

When finally the sun, in a series of Danish riddles from Jutland, is called a ship,[34] the rather elaborate form seems to denote that the source was a book. At all events it raises a rather difficult question. What are the criteria that distinguish a "literary riddle" from the traditional one? One is an over-elaborate description: compare above the rainbow—bridge as given by Schiller, as an extreme instance. Less easy to decide is whether a rather pretty Swedish riddle could be called traditional. It is for the moon—sickle: "Father's scythe is hanging across mother's Sunday skirt." A variation is: "A blue cloth like an altar cloth and a scythe across it."[35] In the absence of any exact criteria, the impression remains that this riddle was designed by an individual; it seems to lack the obvious, self-evident touch that is the hall-mark of a traditional riddle.

The instances quoted, chosen at random from a vast store, could easily be multiplied, and the possibility of so doing is due to the monumental work of Archer Taylor, the first truly effective guide in the maze of versions. Riddles may seem minor items, apparently insignificant, but they are in many ways extremely interesting. Current both in primitive communities and in modern folk tradition everywhere, they have, or seem to have, a different function in each sphere. An interesting problem is the mutual relationship of these functions. The present paper touches upon the question of metaphors in mythology and in riddles. As is shown, the rainbow —bridge and the sun—tree are found in both mythology and riddles, but as far as could be made out by a closer examination, riddles did not borrow from myth; it is more likely that the two sprang from the poetic activities of human creative imagination.

NOTES

1. See B. Malinowski, *The Function of Myth in Primitive Society* (The Frazer Lectures, 1922-32), ed. W. R. Dawson.

2. Thus, in the vast mass of Norwegian traditional legends, the gods—even Tor, the one assumed to have been the most popular —only figure in a single story connected with a huge avalanche of stones which completely blocked the valley. The story was first recorded in 1777.

3. Christian G. Heyne, *Sermonis mythici seu symbolici intrerpretatio* (Göttingen, 1778). For further references see Moltke Moe, "Det mytiske tænkesæt" ["The Mythical Way of Thinking"], *Maal og Minne* (1909).

4. Heinz Werner, "Die Ursprünge der Metapher," *Arbeiten zur Entwicklungspsychologie* (Leipzig, 1919), III, 29.

5. Cf. L. Weiser-Aall, "Der seelische Aufban religiöser Symbole," *Zeitschrift für Volkskunde*, Neue Folge, V, 15ff; and Werner, "Die Ursprünge der Metapher," p. 74ff.

6. In current Norwegian the name in use is *regnbue* 'rainbow,' or, in some dialects, *verbogje* 'weather-bow.' The former name, *regnbogi*, was also used in Ancient Norse, e.g., in sermons as a reference to the Old Testament account of the Deluge; see Stjorn, *The Biblical History of the World in Ancient Norse*, ed. C. R. Unger (Christiania, 1862), p. 62; or a history of the world, appearing in Konrad Gislason, *Prøver av oldnordisk sprog og literatur* (Copenhagen, 1860). The general use of the bow simile was probably due to the biblical story.

7. The version quoted is from W. F. K. Christie, *Norske Gaator* (Bergen, 1868). Further references are: from Eastern Norway— S. Bugge collection, *Norsk Folkekultur*, XI, Supplement (1925) (=Ms., Norsk Folkminnesamling, Delgobe I, 35); from Telemark —S. Bugge, *Norsk Folkekultur*, XI, and R. Berge, *Norsk Visefugg* (Christiania, 1904), p. 253; from Southern Norway—J. Skar, *Gamalt or Sœtesdal* (Christiania, 1916), VIII, 93; from Western

Norway—B. Alver, *Fra Fjon til Fusa* (1950); from Trøndelag—
Publications of the Norsk Folkeminnelag (=NFL), XLII, No. 53;
from Northern Norway—NFL, LIV, 169; from Sweden—H. Ols-
son, *Folkgåtor från Bohuslän* (Uppsala, 1944), No. 350; from Hal-
land—*Vår Bygd* (Halmstad, 1937), p. 12, and Fr. Strøm, *Svenska
Folkgåtor* (Stockholm, 1937), p. 213; from Denmark—E. T. Kristensen, *Danske Folkegaader* (Struer, 1913), No. 445ff.; from Germany—e.g., R. Wossidlo, *Mecklenburgische Volksüberlieferungen*
(Wismar, 1897), I, No. 212: "Hoch erhoben, krumm gebogen,
wunderlich erschaffen. Wer dat raadt, soll aever Nacht bi mi
slapen."

8. Berge, *Norsk Visefugg*, p. 253; cf. *Segner frå bygdom* (Christiania, 1879), III, 126; K. D. Stafset, *280 gamle norske gaator*
(Volden, 1906), No. 17; NFL, XLII, 66; from Sweden—Strøm,
Svenska Folkgåtor, p. 214; Flemish—Moe, "Det mytiske tænkesæt," p. 9. The tree: Schneider Ms., Norsk Folkminnesamling, I,
163; Bugge, *Norsk Folkekultur, XI*, No. 2.

9. Bugge, *Norsk Folkekultur, XI*, No. 4.

10. A. Taylor, "Mongol Riddles," *Proceedings of the American
Philosophical Society*, XLIV (Philadelphia, 1954), No. 854.

11. *Norsk Folkekultur*, XIII, 24; A. Taylor, *English Riddles
from Oral Tradition* (Berkeley and Los Angeles, 1951), p. 302.

12. Moe, "Det mytiske tænkesæt," p. 12.

13. K. Liestøl, "The Draumkvæde, a Norwegian Visionary
Poem from the Middle Ages," *Studia Norvegica* (Oslo, 1946), I,
10, 64.

14. *Am Urquell*, I, 86.

15. *Handwörterbuch der deutschen Aberglaubens*, s.v. *Regenbogen*.

16. Taylor, *English Riddles*, p. 234.

17. Taylor, *English Riddles*, p. 657.

18. Schiller wrote the series, Parabeln und Rätsel, between the
years 1801 and 1804; cf. *Gesammelte Schriften*, ed. Goedecke, II,
351. The first verse was recorded from oral tradition in Sweden
(see Strøm, *Svenska Folkgåtor*, p. 214).

19. Cf. the detailed list of traditional notions about the rainbow
given by Gaidoz in *Melusine, II-V*; and *Handwörterbuch der
deutschen Aberglaubens*, s.v. *Regenbogen*.

20. James G. Frazer, *The Golden Bough*, I, 253; III, 79. The
idea that the rainbow is alive is found also in present day folk-
belief. It is said to be dangerous, and to suck human beings into
itself, where the end touches the ground. It also draws hidden
treasures out of the earth; hence, "the end of the rainbow" is a
likely place to look for such things. J. S. Newberry, in *The Rain-*

bow *Bridge*, has grouped a vast mass of heterogeneous facts around the concept of such a bridge, but his book offers little, if any, relevant information; see a review by H. J. Rose, *Folk-Lore*, XLV (1934), 356.

21. *Edda Snorra Sturlusonar* (Copenhagen, 1848), I, 56.

22. A. Taylor, "Riddles and Poetry," *Southern Folklore Quarterly*, XI (1947), 246: "The subjects of most riddles prevent any poetic emotions from arising. Such prosaic objects as eggs, cows, vegetables, or household objects do not easily lend themselves to a poetic use in the brief compass of a riddle." Cf. the introduction, by J. Sahlgren, to a collection of riddles in *Saga och Säd* (1921-22), p. 25.

23. For variants of such riddles see: Berge, *Norsk Visefugg*, p. 253; NFL, LXVIII, 106; Stafset, *280 gamle norske gaator*, No. 201; from Sweden—Strøm, *Svenska Folkgåtor*, p. 204; from Denmark —Kristensen, *Danske Folkegaader*, Nos. 546ff.; from Ireland— *Béaloideas* (1927), I, 34: "A yellow thread stretched on the side of a house, and nobody can wind it;" cf. *Béaloideas* (1932), III, 350; from Scotland—*Transactions of the Gaelic Society* (Inverness), III, 155; from Iceland—J. Árnason, *Islenzkar Gátur* (Copenhagen, 1887); from Faroe Isles—*Antiquarisk Tidsskrift* (1849-51), p. 315.

24. Norway—NFL, XXXV, 48; Stafset, *280 gamle norske gaator*, No. 203; *Håløygminne* (1924), p. 24. The solution is once said to be the heaven, the sky and the stars: "a golden stick, bending, with more buttons than you could count." Sweden—Strøm, *Svenska Folkgåtor*, p. 207. Denmark—Kristensen, *Danske Folkegaader*, Nos. 545ff.

25. Schwartz, "Der himmlische Lichtbaum," *Zeitschrift für Ethnologie* (1881), p. 139.

26. S. Bugge, *Studier over de nordiske Gude-og Heltesagns oprindelse*, (Christiania, 1881), I, 518.

27. Taylor, *English Riddles*, pp. 18, 194.

28. NFL, I, 148.

29. Strøm, *Svenska Folkgåtor*, p. 204.

30. The Campbell collection, Edinburgh.

31. NFL, VII, 94.

32. Strøm, *Svenska Folkgåtor*, p. 204; cf. Taylor, *English Riddles*, p. 431, and Stafset, *280 gamle norske gaator*, No. 203.

33. Faroe Isles—*Antiquarisk Tidsskrift* (1849-51), p. 315.

34. Kristensen, *Danske Folkegaader*, No. 544a.

35. Strøm, *Svenska Folkgåtor*, p. 210.

THE STRUCTURAL
STUDY OF MYTH

BY CLAUDE LÉVI-STRAUSS

"It would seem that mythological worlds have been built up only to be shattered again, and that new worlds were built from the fragments."—FRANZ BOAS

> Introduction to James Teit, *Traditions of the Thompson River Indians of British Columbia*, Memoirs of the American Folklore Society, VI (1898), 18.

1.0. Despite some recent attempts to renew them, it would seem that during the past twenty years anthropology has more and more turned away from studies in the field of religion. At the same time, and precisely because professional anthropologists' interest has withdrawn from primitive religion, all kinds of amateurs who claim to belong to other disciplines have seized this opportunity to move in, thereby turning into their private playground what we had left as a wasteland. Thus, the prospects for the scientific study of religion have been undermined in two ways.

1.1. The explanation for that situation lies to some extent in the fact that the anthropological study of religion was started by men like Tylor, Frazer, and Durkheim who were psychologically oriented, although not in a position to keep up with the progress of psychological research and theory. Therefore, their interpretations soon became vitiated by the outmoded psychological approach which they used as their backing. Although they were undoubtedly right in giving their attention to intellectual processes, the way they handled them remained so coarse as to discredit them altogether. This is much to be regretted since, as Hocart so profoundly noticed in his introduction to a posthumous book recently published,[1] psychological interpretations were withdrawn from the intellectual field only to be introduced again in the field of affectivity, thus adding to "the inherent defects of the psychological school . . . the mistake of deriving clear-cut ideas . . . from vague emotions." Instead of trying to enlarge the framework of our logic to include processes which, whatever their apparent differences, belong to the same kind of intellectual operations, a naive attempt was made to reduce them to inarticulate emotional drives which resulted only in withering our studies.

1.2. Of all the chapters of religious anthropology probably none has tarried to the same extent as studies in the field of mythology. From a theoretical point of view the situation remains very much the same as it was fifty years ago, namely, a picture of chaos. Myths are still widely interpreted in conflicting ways: collective dreams, the outcome of a kind of esthetic play, the foundation of ritual. . . . Mythological figures are considered as personified abstractions, divinized heroes or decayed gods. Whatever the hypothesis, the choice amounts to reducing mythology either to an idle play or to a coarse kind of speculation.

1.3. In order to understand what a myth really is, are we compelled to choose between platitude and sophism? Some claim that human societies merely express, through their mythology, fundamental feelings common to the whole of mankind, such as love, hate, revenge; or that they try to provide some kind of explanations for phenomena which they cannot understand otherwise: astronomical, meteorological, and the like. But why should these societies do it in such elaborate and devious ways, since all of them are also acquainted with positive explanations? On the other hand, psychoanalysts and many anthropologists have shifted the problems to be explained away from the natural or cosmological towards the sociological and psychological fields. But then the interpretation becomes too easy: if a given mythology confers prominence to a certain character, let us say an evil grandmother, it will be claimed that in such a society grandmothers are actually evil and that mythology reflects the social structure and the social relations; but should the actual data be conflicting, it would be readily claimed that the purpose of mythology is to provide an outlet for repressed feelings. Whatever the situation may be, a clever dialectic will always find a way to pretend that a meaning has been unravelled.

2.0. Mythology confronts the student with a situation which at first sight could be looked upon as contradictory. On the one hand, it would seem that in the course of a myth anything is likely to happen. There is no logic, no continuity. Any characteristic can be attributed to any subject; every conceivable relation can be met. With myth, everything becomes possible. But on the other hand, this apparent arbitrariness is belied by the astounding similarity between myths collected in widely different regions. Therefore the problem: if the content of a myth is contingent, how are we going to explain that throughout the world myths do resemble one another so much?

2.1. It is precisely this awareness of a basic antinomy pertaining to the nature of myth that may lead us towards its solution. For the contradiction which we face is very similar to that which in earlier times brought considerable worry to the first philosophers concerned with linguistic problems; linguistics could only begin to evolve as a science after this contradiction had been overcome. Ancient philosophers were reasoning about language the way we are about mythology. On the one hand, they did notice that in a given language certain sequences of sounds were associated with definite meanings, and they earnestly aimed at discovering a reason for the linkage between those sounds and that meaning. Their attempt, however, was thwarted from the very beginning by the fact that the same sounds were equally present in other languages though the meaning they conveyed was entirely different. The contradiction was surmounted only by the discovery that it is the combination of sounds, not the sounds in themselves, which provides the significant data.

2.2. Now, it is easy to see that some of the more recent interpretations of mythological thought originated from the same kind of misconception under which those early linguists were laboring. Let us consider, for instance, Jung's idea that a given mythological pattern—the so-called archetype—possesses a certain signification. This is comparable to the long supported error that a sound may possess a certain affinity with a meaning: for instance, the "liquid" semi-vowels with water, the open vowels with things that are big, large, loud, or heavy, etc., a kind of theory which still has its supporters.[2] Whatever emendations the original formulation may now call for, everybody will agree that the Saussurean principle of the arbitrary character of the linguistic signs was a prerequisite for the acceding of linguistics to the scientific level.

2.3. To invite the mythologist to compare his precarious situation with that of the linguist in the prescientific stage is not enough. As a matter of fact we may thus be led only from one difficulty to another. There is a very good reason why myth cannot simply be treated as language if its specific problems are to be solved; myth *is* language: to be known, myth has to be told; it is a part of human speech. In order to preserve its specificity we should thus put ourselves in a position to show that it is both the same thing as language, and also something different from it. Here, too, the past experience of linguists may help us. For language itself can be analyzed into things which are at the same time similar and different. This is precisely what is expressed in Saussure's distinction between *langue* and *parole,* one being the structural side of language, the other the statistical aspect of it, *langue* belonging to a revertible time, whereas *parole* is non-revertible. If those two levels already exist in language, then a third one can conceivably be isolated.

2.4. We have just distinguished *langue* and *parole* by the different time referents which they use. Keeping this in mind, we may notice that myth uses a third referent which combines the properties of the first two. On the one hand, a myth always refers to events alleged to have taken place in time: before the world was created, or during its first stages—anyway, long ago. But what gives the myth an operative value is that the specific pattern described is everlasting; it explains the present and the past as well as the future. This can be made clear through a comparison between myth and what appears to have largely replaced it in modern societies, namely, politics. When the historian refers to the French Revolution it is always as a sequence of past happenings, a non-revertible series of events the remote consequences of which may still be felt at present. But to the French politician, as well as to his followers, the French Revolution is both a sequence belonging to the past—as to the historian—and an everlasting pattern which can be detected in the present French social structure and which provides a clue for its interpretation, a lead from which to infer the future developments. See, for instance, Michelet who was a politically-minded historian. He describes the French Revolution thus: "This day . . . everything was possible. . . . Future became present . . . that is, no more time, a glimpse of eternity." It is that double structure, altogether historical and anhistorical, which explains that myth, while pertaining to the realm of the *parole* and calling for an explanation as such, as well as to that of the *langue* in which it is expressed, can also be an absolute object on a third level which, though it remains linguistic by nature, is nevertheless distinct from the other two.

2.5. A remark can be introduced at this point which will help to show the singularity of myth among other linguistic phenomena. Myth is the part of language where the formula *traduttore, traditore* reaches its lowest truth-value. From that point of view it should be put in the whole gamut of linguistic expressions at the end opposite to that of poetry, in spite of all the claims which have been made to prove the contrary. Poetry is a kind of speech which cannot be translated except at the cost of serious distortions; whereas the mythical value of the myth remains preserved, even through the worst translation. Whatever our ignorance of the language and the culture of the people where it originated, a myth is still felt as a myth by any reader throughout the world. Its substance does not lie in its style, its original music, or its syntax, but in the *story* which it tells. It is language, functioning on an especially high level where meaning succeeds practically at "taking off" from the linguistic ground on which it keeps on rolling.

2.6. To sum up the discussion at this point, we have so far made the following claims: 1. If there is a meaning to be found in mythology, this cannot reside in the isolated elements which enter into the composition of a myth, but only in the way those elements are combined. 2. Although myth belongs to the same category as language, being, as a matter of fact, only part of it, language in myth unveils specific properties. 3. Those properties are only to be found *above* the ordinary linguistic level; that is, they exhibit more complex features beside those which are to be found in any kind of linguistic expression.

3.0. If the above three points are granted, at least as a working hypothesis, two consequences will follow: 1. Myth, like the rest of language, is made up of constituent units. 2. These constituent units presuppose the constituent units present in language when analyzed on other levels, namely, phonemes, morphemes, and semantemes, but they, nevertheless, differ from the latter in the same was as they themselves differ from morphemes, and these from phonemes; they belong to a higher order, a more complex one. For this reason, we will call them *gross constituent units*.

3.1. How shall we proceed in order to identify and isolate these gross constituent units? We know that they cannot be found among phonemes, morphemes, or semantemes, but only on a higher level; otherwise myth would become confused with any other kind of speech. Therefore, we should look for them on the sentence level. The only method we can suggest at this stage is to proceed tentatively, by trial and error, using as a check the principles which serve as a basis for any kind of structural analysis: economy of explanation; unity of solution; and ability to reconstruct the whole from a fragment, as well as further stages from previous ones.

3.2. The technique which has been applied so far by this writer consists in analyzing each myth individually, breaking down its story into the shortest possible sentences, and writing each such sentence on an index card bearing a number corresponding to the unfolding of the story.

3.3. Practically each card will thus show that a certain function is, at a given time, predicated to a given subject. Or, to put it otherwise, each gross constituent unit will consist in a relation.

3.4. However, the above definition remains highly unsatisfactory for two different reasons. In the first place, it is well known to structural linguists that constituent units on all levels are made up of relations and the true difference between our gross units and the others stays unexplained; moreover, we still find ourselves in the realm of a non-revertible time since the numbers of the cards correspond to the unfolding of the informant's speech. Thus, the specific character of mythological time, which as we have seen is both revertible and non-revertible, synchronic and diachronic, remains unaccounted for. Therefrom comes a new hypothesis which constitutes the very core of our argument: the true constituent units of a myth are not the isolated relations but *bundles of such relations* and it is only as bundles that these relations can be put to use and combined so as to produce a meaning. Relations pertaining to the same bundle may appear diachronically at remote intervals, but when we have succeeded in grouping them together, we have reorganized our myth according to a time referent of a new nature corresponding to the prerequisite of the initial hypothesis, namely, a two-dimensional time referent which is simultaneously diachronic and synchronic and which accordingly integrates the characteristics of the *langue* on one hand, and those of the *parole* on the other. To put it in even more linguistic terms, it is as though a phoneme were always made up of all its variants.

4.0. Two comparisons may help to explain what we have in mind.

4.1. Let us first suppose that archaeologists of the future coming from another planet would one day, when all human life had disappeared from the earth, excavate one of our libraries. Even if they were at first ignorant of our writing, they might succeed in deciphering it—an undertaking which would require, at some early stage, the discovery that the alphabet, as we are in the habit of printing it, should be read from left to right and from top to bottom. However, they would soon find out that a whole category of books did not fit the usual pattern: these would be the orchestra scores on the shelves of the music division. But after trying, without success, to decipher staffs one after the other, from the upper down to the lower, they would probably notice that the same patterns of notes recurred at intervals, either in full or in part, or that some patterns were strongly reminiscent of earlier ones. Hence the hypothesis: what if patterns showing affinity, instead of being considered in succession, were to be treated as one complex pattern and read globally? By getting at what we call *harmony*, they would then find out that an orchestra score, in order to become meaningful, has to be read diachronically along one axis—that is, page after page, and from left to right—and also synchronically along the other axis, all the notes which are written vertically making up one gross constituent unit, i.e. one bundle of relations.

4.2. The other comparison is somewhat different. Let us take an observer ignorant of our playing cards, sitting for a long time with a fortune-teller. He would know something of the visitors: sex, age, look, social situation, etc. in the same way as we know something of the different cultures whose myths we try to study. He would also listen to the séances and keep them recorded so as to be able to go over them and make comparisons—as we do when we listen to myth telling and record it. Mathematicians to whom I have put the problem agree that if the man is bright and if the material available to him is sufficient, he may be able to reconstruct the nature of the deck of cards being used, that is: fifty-two or thirty-two cards according to case, made up of four homologous series consisting of the same units (the individual cards) with only one varying feature, the suit.

4.3. The time has come to give a concrete example of the method we propose. We will use the Oedipus myth which has the advantage of being well-known to everybody and for which no preliminary explanation is therefore needed. By doing so, I am well aware that the Oedipus myth has only reached us under late forms and through literary transfigurations concerned more with esthetic and moral preoccupations than with religious or ritual ones, whatever these may have been. But as will be shown later, this apparently unsatisfactory situation will strengthen our demonstration rather than weaken it.

4.4. The myth will be treated as would be an orchestra score perversely presented as a unilinear series and where our task is to re-establish the correct disposition. As if, for instance, we were confronted with a sequence of the type: 1,2,4,7,8,2,3,4,6,8,1,4,5,7,8,1,2,5,7,3,4,5,6,8 . . . , the assignment being to put all the 1's together, all the 2's, the 3's, etc.; the result is a chart:

1	2		4			7	8
	2	3	4		6		8
1			4	5		7	8
1	2			5		7	
		3	4	5			
					6		8

4.5. We will attempt to perform the same kind of operation on the Oedipus myth, trying out several dispositions until we find one which is in harmony with the principles enumerated under 3.1. Let us suppose, for the sake of argument, that the best arrangement is the following (although it might certainly be improved by the help of a specialist in Greek mythology):

Kadmos seeks his sister Europa ravished by Zeus		
		Kadmos kills the dragon
	The Spartoi kill each other	
		Labdacos (Laios' father) = *lame* (?)
	Oedipus kills his father Laios	Laios (Oedipus' father) = *left-sided* (?)

		Oedipus kills the Sphinx	
Oedipus marries his mother Jocasta	Eteocles kills his brother Polynices		Oedipus = *swollen-foot* (?)
Antigone buries her brother Polynices despite prohibition			

4.6. Thus, we find ourselves confronted with four vertical columns each of which include several relations belonging to the same bundle. Were we to *tell* the myth, we would disregard the columns and read the rows from left to right and from top to bottom. But if we want to *understand* the myth, then we will have to disregard one half of the diachronic dimension (top to bottom) and read from left to right, column after column, each one being considered as a unit.

4.7. All the relations belonging to the same column exhibit one common feature which it is our task to unravel. For instance, all the events grouped in the first column on the left have something to do with blood relations which are overemphasized, i.e. are subject to a more intimate treatment than they should be. Let us say, then, that the first column has as its common feature the *overrating of blood relations*. It is obvious that the second column expresses the same thing, but inverted: *underrating of blood relations*. The third column refers to monsters being slain. As to the fourth, a word of clarification is needed. The remarkable connotation of the surnames in Oedipus' father-line has often been noticed. However, linguists usually disregard it, since to them the only way to define the meaning of a term is to investigate all the contexts in which it appears, and personal names, precisely because they are used as such, are not accompanied by any context. With the method we propose to follow the objection disappears since the myth itself provides its own context. The meaningful fact is no longer to be looked for in the eventual sense of each name, but in the fact that all the names have a common feature: i.e. that they may eventually mean something and that all these hypothetical meanings (which may well remain hypothetical) exhibit a common feature, namely they refer to *difficulties to walk and to behave straight*.

4.8. What is then the relationship between the two columns on the right? Column three refers to monsters. The dragon is a chthonian being which has to be killed in order that mankind be born from the earth; the Sphinx is a monster unwilling to permit men to live. The last unit reproduces the first one which has to do with the *autochthonous origin* of mankind. Since the monsters are overcome by men, we may thus say that the common feature of the third column is *the denial of the autochthonous origin of man*.

4.9. This immediately helps us to understand the meaning of the fourth column. In mythology it is a universal character of men born from the earth that at the moment they emerge from the depth, they either cannot walk or do it clumsily. This is the case of the chthonian beings in the mythology of the Pueblo: Masauwu, who leads the emergence, and the chthonian Shumaikoli are lame ("bleeding-foot," "sore-foot"). The same happens to the Koskimo of the Kwakiutl after they have been swallowed by the chthonian monster, Tsiakish: when they returned to the surface of the earth "they limped forward or tripped sideways." Then the common feature of the fourth column is: *the persistence of the autochthonous origin of man*. It follows that column four is to column three as column one is to column two. The inability to connect two kinds of relationships is overcome (or rather replaced) by the positive statement that contradictory relationships are identical inasmuch as they are both self-contradictory in a similar way. Although this is still a provisional formulation of the structure of mythical thought, it is sufficient at this stage.

4.10. Turning back to the Oedipus myth, we may now see what it means. The myth has to do with the inability, for a culture which holds the belief that mankind is autochthonous (see, for instance, Pausanias, VIII, xxix, 4: vegetals provide a *model* for humans), to find a satisfactory transition between this theory and the knowledge that human beings are actually born from the union of man and woman. Although the problem obviously cannot be solved, the Oedipus myth provides a kind of logical tool which, to phrase it coarsely, replaces the original problem: born from one or born from two? born from different or born from same? By a correlation of this type, the overrating of blood relations is to the underrating of blood relations as the attempt to escape autochthony is to the impossibility to succeed in it. Although experience contradicts theory, social life verifies the cosmology by its similarity of structure. Hence cosmology is true.

4.11.0. Two remarks should be made at this stage.

4.11.1. In order to interpret the myth, we were able to leave aside a point which has until now worried the specialists, namely, that in the earlier (Homeric) versions of the Oedipus myth, some basic elements are lacking, such as Jocasta killing herself and Oedipus piercing his own eyes. These events do not alter the substance of the myth although they can easily be integrated, the first one as a new case of autodestruction (column three) while the second is another case of crippledness (column four). At the same time there is something significant in these additions since the shift from foot to head is to be correlated with the shift from: autochthonous origin negated to: self-destruction.

4.11.2. Thus, our method eliminates a problem which has been so far one of the main obstacles to the progress of mythological studies, namely, the quest for the *true* version, or the *earlier* one. On the contrary, we define the myth as consisting of all its versions; to put it otherwise: a myth remains the same as long as it is felt as such. A striking example is offered by the fact that our interpretation may take into account, and is certainly applicable to, the Freudian use of the Oedipus myth. Although the Freudian problem has ceased to be that of autochthony *versus* bisexual reproduction, it is still the problem of understanding how *one* can be born from *two*: how is it that we do not have only one procreator, but a mother plus a father? Therefore, not only Sophocles, but Freud himself, should be included among the recorded versions of the Oedipus myth on a par with earlier or seemingly more "authentic" versions.

5.0. An important consequence follows. If a myth is made up of all its variants, structural analysis should take all of them into account. Thus, after analyzing all the known variants of the Theban version, we should treat the others in the same way: first, the tales about Labdacos' collateral line including Agavé, Pentheus, and Jocasta herself; the Theban variant about Lycos with Amphion and Zetos as the city founders; more remote variants concerning Dionysos (Oedipus' matrilaterial cousin), and Athenian legends where Cecrops takes the place of Kadmos, etc. For each of them a similar chart should be drawn, and then compared and reorganized according to the findings: Cecrops killing the serpent with the parallel episode of Kadmos: abandonment of Dionysos with abandonment of Oedipus; "Swollen Foot" with Dionysos *loxias*, i.e. walking obliquely; Europa's quest with Antiope's; the foundation of Thebes by the Spartoi or by the brothers Amphion and Zetos; Zeus kidnapping Europa and Antiope and the same with Semele; the Theban Oedipus and the Argian Perseus, etc. We will then have several two-dimensional charts, each dealing with a variant, to be organized in a three-dimensional order

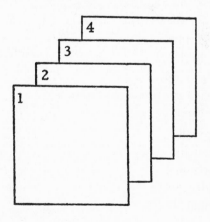

FIG. 1

so that three different readings become possible: left to right, top to bottom, front to back. All of these charts cannot be expected to be identical; but experience shows that any difference to be observed may be correlated with other differences, so that a logical treatment of the whole will allow simplifications, the final outcome being the structural law of the myth.

5.1. One may object at this point that the task is impossible to perform since we can only work with known versions. Is it not possible that a new version might alter the picture? This is true enough if only one or two versions are available, but the objection becomes theoretical as soon as a reasonably large number has been recorded (a number which experience will progressively tell, at least as an approximation). Let us make this point clear by a comparison. If the furniture of a room and the way it is arranged in the room were known to us only through its reflection in two mirrors placed on opposite walls, we would theoretically dispose of an almost infinite number of mirror-images which would provide us with a complete knowledge. However, should the two mirrors be obliquely set, the number of mirror-images would become very small; nevertheless, four or five such images would very likely give us, if not complete information, at least a sufficient coverage so that we would feel sure that no large piece of furniture is missing in our description.

5.2. On the other hand, it cannot be too strongly emphasized that all available variants should be taken into account. If Freudian comments on the Oedipus complex are a part of the Oedipus myth, then questions such as whether Cushing's version of the Zuni origin myth should be retained or discarded become irrelevant. There is no one true version of which all the others are but copies or distortions. Every version belongs to the myth.

5.3. Finally it can be understood why works on general mythology have given discouraging results. This comes from two reasons. First, comparative mythologists have picked up preferred versions instead of using them all. Second, we have seen that the structural analysis of *one* variant of *one* myth belonging to *one* tribe (in some cases, even *one* village) already requires two dimensions. When we use several variants of the same myth for the same tribe or village, the frame of reference becomes three-dimensional and as soon as we try to enlarge the comparison, the number of dimensions required increases to such an extent that it appears quite impossible to handle them intuitively. The confusions and platitudes which are the outcome of comparative mythology can be explained by the fact that multi-dimensional frames of reference cannot be ignored, or naively replaced by two- or three-dimensional ones. Indeed, progress in comparative mythology depends largely on the cooperation of mathematicians who would undertake to express in symbols multi-dimensional relations which cannot be handled otherwise.

6.0. In order to check this theory,[3] an attempt was made in 1953-54 towards an exhaustive analysis of all the known versions of the Zuni origin and emergence myth: Cushing, 1883 and 1896; Stevenson, 1904; Parsons, 1923; Bunzel, 1932; Benedict, 1934. Furthermore, a preliminary attempt was made at a comparison of the results with similar myths in other Pueblo tribes, Western and Eastern. Finally, a test was undertaken with Plains mythology. In all cases, it was found that the theory was sound, and light was thrown, not only on North American mythology, but also on a previously unnoticed kind of logical operation, or one known only so far in a wholly different context. The bulk of material which needs to be handled almost at the beginning of the work makes it impossible to enter into details, and we will have to limit ourselves here to a few illustrations.

6.1. An over-simplified chart of the Zuni emergence myth would read as follows:

INCREASE			DEATH
mechanical growth of vegetals (used as ladders)	emergence led by Beloved Twins	sibling incest	gods kill children
food value of wild plants	migration led by the two Newekwe		magical contest with people of the dew (collecting wild food *versus* cultivation)
		sibling sacrificed (to gain victory)	

food value of cultivated plants			
		sibling adopted (in exchange for corn)	
periodical character of agricultural work			
			war against Kyanakwe (gardeners *versus* hunters)
hunting	war led by two war-gods		
			salvation of the tribe (center of the world found)
warfare		sibling sacrificed (to avoid flood)	

DEATH   PERMANENCY

6.2. As may be seen from a global inspection of the chart, the basic problem consists in discovering a mediation between life and death. For the Pueblo, the problem is especially difficult since they understand the origin of human life on the model of vegetal life (emergence from the earth). They share that belief with the ancient Greeks, and it is not without reason that we chose the Oedipus myth as our first example. But in the American case, the highest form of vegetal life is to be found in agriculture which is periodical in nature, i.e. which consists in an alternation between life and death. If this is disregarded, the contradiction surges at another place: agriculture provides food, therefore life; but hunting provides food and is similar to warfare which means death. Hence there are three different ways of handling the problem. In the Cushing version, the difficulty revolves around an opposition between activities yielding an immediate result (collecting wild food) and activities yielding a delayed result—death has to become integrated so that agriculture can exist. Parsons' version goes from hunting to agriculture, while Stevenson's version operates the other way around. It can be shown that all the differences between these versions can be rigorously correlated with these basic structures. For instance:

		CUSHING	PARSONS	STEVENSON
Gods	⎫	allied, use fiber strings on their bows (gardeners)	Kyanakwe alone, use fiber string	Gods ⎱ allied, use
Kyanakwe	⎭			Men ⎰ fiber string

	VICTORIOUS OVER	VICTORIOUS OVER	VICTORIOUS OVER
Men	alone, use sinew (hunters) (until men shift to fiber)	Gods ⎱ allied, use Men ⎰ sinew string	Kyanakwe alone, use sinew string

Since fiber strings (vegetal) are always superior to sinew strings (animal) and since (to a lesser extent) the gods' alliance is preferable to their antagonism, it follows that in Cushing's version, men begin to be doubly underprivileged (hostile gods, sinew string); in Stevenson, doubly privileged (friendly gods, fiber string); while Parsons' version confronts us with an intermediary situation (friendly gods, but sinew strings since men begin by being hunters). Hence:

	CUSHING	PARSONS	STEVENSON
gods/men	−	+	+
fiber/sinew	−	−	+

6.3. Bunzel's version is from a structural point of view of the same type as Cushing's. However, it differs from both Cushing's and Stevenson's inasmuch as the latter two explain the emergence as a result of man's need to evade his pitiful condition, while Bunzel's version makes it the consequence of a call from the higher powers—hence the inverted sequences of the means restored to for the emergence: in both

Cushing and Stevenson, they go from plant to animals; in Bunzel, from mammals to insects and from insects to plants.

6.4. Among the Western Pueblo the logical approach always remains the same; the starting point and the point of arrival are the simplest ones and ambiguity is met halfway:

The Structural Study of Myth

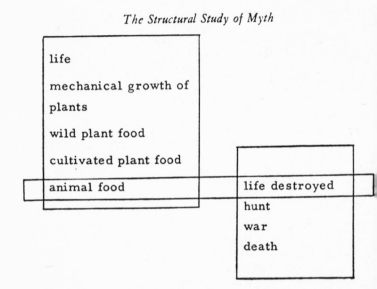

FIG. 2

The fact that contradiction appears in the middle of the dialectical process has as its result the production of a double series of dioscuric pairs the purpose of which is to operate a mediation between conflicting terms:

1. 3 divine messengers   2 ceremonial clowns   2 war-gods

2. homogeneous pair: siblings (brother   couple
   dioscurs (2 brothers)   and sister)   (husband
                                                      and wife)
       heterogeneous pair: grandmother/grandchild

which consists in combinatory variants of the same function; (hence the war attribute of the clowns which has given rise to so many queries).

6.5 Some Central and Eastern Pueblos proceed the other way around. They begin by stating the identity of hunting and cultivation (first corn obtained by Game-Father sowing deer-dewclaws), and they try to derive both life and death from that central notion. Then, instead of extreme terms being simple and intermediary ones duplicated as among the Western groups, the extreme terms become duplicated (i.e., the two sisters of the Eastern Pueblo) while a simple mediating term comes to the foreground (for instance, the Poshaiyanne of the Zia), but endowed with equivocal attributes. Hence the attributes of this "messiah" can be deduced from the place it occupies in the time sequence: good when at the beginning (Zuni, Cushing), equivocal in the middle (Central Pueblo), bad at the end (Zia), except in Bunzel where the sequence is reversed as has been shown.

6.6 By using systematically this kind of structural analysis it becomes possible to organize all the known variants of a myth as a series forming a kind of permutation group, the two variants placed at the far-ends being in a symmetrical, though inverted, relationship to each other.

7.0 Our method not only has the advantage of bringing some kind of order to what was previously chaos; it also enables us to perceive some basic logical processes which are at the root of mythical thought. Three main processes should be distinguished.

7.1.0 The trickster of American mythology has remained so far a problematic figure. Why is it that throughout North America his part is assigned practically everywhere to either coyote or raven? If we keep in mind that mythical thought always works from the awareness of oppositions towards their progressive mediation, the reason for those choices becomes clearer. We need only to assume that two opposite terms with no intermediary always tend to be replaced by two equivalent terms which allow a third one as a mediator; then one of the polar terms and the mediator becomes replaced by a new triad and so on. Thus we have:

INITIAL PAIR	FIRST TRIAD	SECOND TRIAD
Life		
	Agriculture	
		Herbivorous animals
		Carrion-eating animals (raven; coyote)
	Hunt	
		Prey animals
	War	
Death		

With the unformulated argument: carrion-eating animals are like prey animals (they eat animal food), but they are also like food-plant producers (they do not kill what they eat). Or, to put it otherwise, Pueblo style: ravens are to gardens as prey animals are to herbivorous ones. But it is also clear that herbivorous animals may be called first to act as mediators on the assumption that they are like collectors and gatherers (vegetal-food eaters) while they can be used as animal food though not themselves hunters. Thus we may have mediators of the first order, of the second order, and so on, where each term gives birth to the next by a double process of opposition and correlation.

7.1.1. This kind of process can be followed in the mythology of the Plains where we may order the data according to the sequence:

Unsuccessful mediator between earth and sky
(Star husband's wife)

Heterogeneous pair of mediators
(grandmother/grandchild)

Semi-homogeneous pair of mediators
(Lodge-Boy and Thrown-away)

While among the Pueblo we have:

> Successful mediator between earth and sky
> (Poshaiyanki)
>
> Semi-homogeneous pair of mediators
> (Uyuyewi and Matsailema)
>
> Homogenous pair of mediators
> (the Ahaiyuta)

7.1.2. On the other hand, correlations may appear on a transversal axis (this is true even on the linguistic level; see the manifold connotation of the root *pose* in Tewa according to Parsons: coyote, mist, scalp, etc.). Coyote is intermediary between herbivorous and carnivorous in the same way as mist between sky and earth; scalp between war and hunt (scalp is war-crop); corn smut between wild plants and cultivated plants; garments between "nature" and "culture"; refuse between village and outside; ashes between roof and hearth (chimney). This string of mediators, if one may call them so, not only throws light on whole pieces of North American mythology—why the Dew-God may be at the same time the Game-Master and the giver of raiments and be personified as an "Ash-Boy"; or why the scalps are mist producing; or why the Game-Mother is associated with corn smut; etc.—but it also probably corresponds to a universal way of organizing daily experience. See, for instance, the French for vegetal smut; *nielle,* from Latin *nebula;* the luck-bringing power attributed to refuse (old shoe) and ashes (kissing chimney-sweepers); and compare the American Ash-Boy cycle with the Indo-European Cinderella: both phallic figures (mediator between male and female); master of the dew and of the game; owners of fine raiments; and social bridges (low class marrying into high class); though impossible to interpret through recent diffusion as has been sometimes contended since Ash-Boy and Cinderella are symmetrical but inverted in every detail (while the borrowed Cinderella tale in America—Zuni Turkey-Girl—is parallel to the prototype):

	EUROPE	AMERICA
Sex	female	male
Family Status	double family	no family
Appearance	pretty girl	ugly boy
Sentimental status	nobody likes her	in hopeless love with girl
Transformation	luxuriously clothed with supernatural help	stripped of ugliness with supernatural help

etc.

7.2.0. Thus, the mediating function of the trickster explains that since its position is halfway between two polar terms he must retain something of that duality, namely an ambiguous and equivocal character. But the trickster figure is not the only conceivable form of mediation; some myths seem to devote themselves to the task of exhausting all the possible solutions to the problem of bridging the gap between *two* and *one*. For instance, a comparison between all the variants of the Zuni emergence myth provides us with a series of mediating devices, each of which creates the next one by a process of opposition and correlation:

$$\text{messiah} > \text{dioscurs} > \text{trickster} > \frac{\text{bisexual}}{\text{being}} > \frac{\text{sibling}}{\text{pair}} >$$

$$\frac{\text{married}}{\text{couple}} > \frac{\text{grandmother-}}{\text{grandchild}} > \frac{\text{4 terms}}{\text{group}} > \text{triad}$$

In Cushing's version, this dialectic is accompanied by a change from the space dimension (mediating between sky and earth) to the time dimension (mediating between summer and winter, i.e., between birth and death). But while the shift is being made from space to time, the final solution (triad) re-introduces space, since a triad consists in a dioscur pair *plus* a messiah simultaneously present; and while the point of departure was ostensibly formulated in terms of a

space referent (sky and earth) this was nevertheless implicitly conceived in terms of a time referent (first the messiah
calls; *then* the dioscurs descend). Therefore the logic of myth
confronts us with a double, reciprocal exchange of functions
to which we shall return shortly (7.3.).

7.2.1. Not only can we account for the ambiguous character of the trickster, but we may also understand another
property of mythical figures the world over, namely, that
the same god may be endowed with contradictory attributes;
for instance, he may be *good* and *bad* at the same time. If
we compare the variants of the Hopi myth of the origin of
Shalako, we may order them so that the following structure
becomes apparent:

$$(\text{Masauwu: } x) \simeq (\text{Muyingwu: Masauwu}) \simeq$$
$$(\text{Shalako: Muyingwu}) \simeq (y\text{: Masauwu})$$

where x and y represent arbitrary values corresponding to
the fact that in the two "extreme" variants the god Masauwu,
while appearing alone instead of associated with another god,
as in variant two, or being absent, as in three, still retains intrinsically a relative value. In variant one, Masauwu (alone)
is depicted as helpful to mankind (though not as helpful as
he could be), and in version four, harmful to mankind
(though not as harmful as he could be); whereas in two,
Muyingwu is relatively more helpful than Masauwu, and in
three, Shalako more helpful than Muyingwu. We find an
identical series when ordering the Keresan variants.

$$(\text{Poshaiyanki: } x) \simeq (\text{Lea: Poshaiyanki}) \simeq$$
$$(\text{Poshaiyanki: Tiamoni}) \simeq (y\text{: Poshaiyanki})$$

7.2.2. This logical framework is particularly interesting
since sociologists are already acquainted with it on two other
levels: first, with the problem of the pecking order among
hens; and second, it also corresponds to what this writer has
called *general exchange* in the field of kinship. By recognizing it also on the level of mythical thought, we may find ourselves in a better position to appraise its basic importance in
sociological studies and to give it a more inclusive theoretical
interpretation.

7.3.0. Finally, when we have succeeded in organizing a whole series of variants in a kind of permutation group, we are in a position to formulate the law of that group. Although it is not possible at the present stage to come closer than an approximate formulation which will certainly need to be made more accurate in the future, it seems that every myth (considered as the collection of all its variants) corresponds to a formula of the following type:

$$f_x(a) : f_y(b) \simeq f_x(b) : f_a - 1(y)$$

where, two terms being given as well as two functions of these terms, it is stated that a relation of equivalence still exists between two situations when terms and relations are inverted, under two conditions: 1. that one term be replaced by its contrary; 2. that an inversion be made between the *function* and the *term* value of two elements.

7.3.1. This formula becomes highly significant when we recall that Freud considered that *two traumas* (and not one as it is so commonly said) are necessary in order to give birth to this individual myth in which a neurosis consists. By trying to apply the formula to the analysis of those traumatisms (and assuming that they correspond to conditions 1. and 2. respectively) we should not only be able to improve it, but would find ourselves in the much desired position of developing side by side the sociological and the psychological aspects of the theory; we may also take it to the laboratory and subject it to experimental verification.

8.0. At this point it seems unfortunate that, with the limited means at the disposal of French anthropological research, no further advance can be made. It should be emphasized that the task of analyzing mythological literature, which is extremely bulky, and of breaking it down into its constituent units, requires team work and secretarial help. A variant of average length needs several hundred cards to be properly analyzed. To discover a suitable pattern of rows and columns for those cards, special devices are needed, consisting of vertical boards about two meters long and one and one-half meters high, where cards can be pigeon-holed and moved at will; in order to build up three-dimensional models enabling

one to compare the variants, several such boards are necessary, and this in turn requires a spacious workshop, a kind
of commodity particularly unavailable in Western Europe
nowadays. Furthermore, as soon as the frame of reference
becomes multi-dimensional (which occurs at an early stage,
as has been shown in 5.3.) the board-system has to be replaced by perforated cards which in turn require I.B.M.
equipment, etc. Since there is little hope that such facilities
will become available in France in the near future, it is much
desired that some American group, better equipped than we
are here in Paris, will be induced by this paper to start a
project of its own in structural mythology.

8.1.0. Three final remarks may serve as conclusion.

8.1.1. First, the question has often been raised why myths,
and more generally oral literature, are so much addicted to
duplication, triplication or quadruplication of the same sequence. If our hypotheses are accepted, the answer is obvious: repetition has as its function to make the structure of the
myth apparent. For we have seen that the synchro-diachroni-
cal sructure of the myth permits us to organize it into dia-
chronical sequences (the rows in our tables) which should be
read synchronically (the columns). Thus, a myth exhibits a
"slated" structure which seeps to the surface, if one may say
so, through the repetition process.

8.1.2. However, the slates are not absolutely identical to
each other. And since the purpose of myth is to provide a
logical model capable of overcoming a contradiction (an impossible achievement if, as it happens, the contradicition is
real), a theoretically infinite number of slates will be gen-
erated, each one slightly different from the others. Thus,
myth grows spiral-wise until the intellectual impulse which
has originated it is exhausted. Its growth is a continuous process whereas its structure remains discontinuous. If this is
the case we should consider that it closely corresponds, in the
realm of the spoken word, to the kind of being a crystal is in
the realm of physical matter. This analogy may help us understand better the relationship of myth on one hand to both
langue and *parole* on the other.

8.1.3. Prevalent attempts to explain alleged differences between the so-called "primitive" mind and scientific thought

have resorted to qualitative differences between the working processes of the mind in both cases while assuming that the objects to which they were applying themselves remained very much the same. If our interpretation is correct, we are led toward a completely different view, namely, that the kind of logic which is used by mythical thought is as rigorous as that of modern science, and that the difference lies not in the quality of the intellectual process, but in the nature of the things to which it is applied. This is well in agreement with the situation known to prevail in the field of technology: what makes a steel ax superior to a stone one is not that the first one is better made than the second. They are equally well made, but steel is a different thing than stone. In the same way we may be able to show that the same logical processes are put to use in myth as in science, and that man has always been thinking equally well; the improvement lies, not in an alleged progress of man's conscience, but in the discovery of new things to which it may apply its unchangeable abilities.

NOTES

1. A. M. Hocart, *Social Origins* (London, 1954), p. 7.

2. See, for instance, Sir R. A. Paget, "The Origin of Language . . . ," *Journal of World History*, I, No. 2 (UNESCO, 1953).

3. Thanks are due to an unsolicited, but deeply appreciated, grant from the Ford Foundation.

THE PERSONAL USE
OF MYTH IN DREAMS

BY DOROTHY EGGAN

THROUGHOUT their development folklore and ethnology have used reciprocal kinship terms in addressing one another, but for the most part each, absorbed in the task of becoming a science, has used similar data for different goals, and the relationship has not been sufficiently exploited. Recently, however, Stith Thompson has asked some significant questions regarding the relations between an individual and his folklore,[1] a subject in which anthropologists, too, have become increasingly interested. This paper is an attempt to illustrate some of these interactions. The first section sketches some anthropological thinking pertinent to the problem; the second uses data from a collection of Hopi Indian dreams[2] to illustrate how one individual, caught in a conflict—both internal and external—between his ambivalent desire to be *bahana* (White) and to be a good Hopi, resenting his inadequacy as a hunter and runner, concerned with the quality of his courage and with problems in his sexual life, uses Hopi myths[3] to fuse his personal problems with those of his culture's heroes, thus reducing his own anxiety about them. We are fortunate in having at our disposal for this purpose a comprehensive body of Hopi myths and folktales, including a volume of lore collected by Voth during the informant's childhood and in his village.[4]

The anthropologist has frequently employed folklorists' techniques to deepen his understanding of culture, and in so doing has called attention to the individual as a third dimension of the triangle.[5] Boas, pioneering in this experiment, used mythology to analyze the historic determination and diffusion of certain culture traits. But he also found, as psychological by-products of his examination of Tsimshian mythology, the characteristic way in which imagination gives reality to wishes, exaggerates experiences and materializes fears, or creates situations contrary to daily experience; and he suggested that imagination being limited, people prefer to operate with the old stock of imaginative happenings rather than to invent new ones.[6]

More recently Lantis discusses the universal desire to transcend human limitations, the common *subjective* experience derived from the sharing by a people of a body of folklore, and cites among other positive functions of mythology the relief from anxiety which it affords. Thus she, too, from a detailed examination of Nunivak Eskimo mythology, sees in the analysis of folklore, not only clues to the origin and delineation of aspects of culture, but she also raises specific questions about what this cultural heritage *says to the individual* who uses it in his daily life.[7]

Kluckhohn lists ways in which myths and rituals protect "cultural continuity" and "stabilize society," but also asks "how are myths and rituals rewarding enough in the daily lives of individuals" so that they "continue to prevail at the expense of more rational responses?" In sketching a tentative series of working hypotheses with which to approach this question he points out the way in which emotions, seeking discharge, seize upon culturally supplied sanctions which are emotionally charged, to—among other things—reduce the individual's "anticipation of disaster;" how, in short, these cultural manifestations are used by the ego as "mechanisms of defense" in accordance with "psychoanalytic principles."[8]

Important for an understanding of this interaction between an individual and his social heritage is a consideration of the process as such, and the *affects* involved in specific learning experiences. Among the Hopi, children were seldom expected to learn by rote. Rather they learned in associated patterns[9] from teachers who saw all aspects of existence woven together in meaningful form. Elsewhere I have discussed the affects concomitant with the learning situation among the Hopi.[10] Summarizing briefly for the purposes of this paper we find that in addition to careful, deliberate instruction in every phase of Hopi life, myths, dreams and actual experiences were told and retold, for both *fantasy and story-telling* had a *vital role* in the Hopi world. Around the communal bowl, in the kiva—everywhere this form of teaching went on, and on such occasions the feeling of solidarity within the group was normally very strong, for in reaffirmation, faith in all things Hopi was renewed. Surrounded by the affection and security of an intimate group, with few outside experiences to modify the impact until they were sent to an alien school, children learned Hopi tradition from people who believed implicitly in what they taught and thus conveyed conviction through their teaching. And they learned it in the Hopi language which has, as Whorf has said, its own characteristic "ways of analyzing and reporting experience."[11]

In the past this method of socialization among the Hopi was a surprisingly effective substitute for theater, church, school, and jail; and for the teachers it was to a very real extent a substitute also for the psychoanalytic couch, since in reaffirmation, restatement, and reliving of beliefs and experiences, much doubt and bitterness was worked out. For the learners, related patterns of Hopi philosophy and behavior were absorbed in an *emotionally charged atmosphere* which tended to *fuse reality and fantasy,* and to make the resulting patterns more rewarding for "ego-synthesis"[12] than were the hard reality responses, which, when observed from our conceptions of logic, seem to us more rational. So insofar as an individual became adequately socialized from the viewpoint of his society—which the long history of cultural stability among the Hopi indicates that most individuals were—he tended to store in his memory related items which were representative of the group's thought processes.[13]

Even in the realm of imagination then, including folklore

and dreams, thinking processes are not only limited by one's language and perception, but are also stimulated by them. Therefore culture and creativity cannot be examined separately for, as Herskovits expresses it, "The creative life does not lie outside the influence of the enculturative experience." On the contrary, "in his experimentation" the artist is "unwittingly" guided by it.[14]

Since we here deal with one man's manipulation of "socialized fantasy," we shall now reverse Kluckhohn's statement that when an individual fantasy becomes congenial to a group it becomes myth,[15] and assert that when a myth is congenial enough to the individual he may use it as personal fantasy. For in the learning process discussed above an individual tends to remember most clearly, to adapt, and subsequently to restate or reflect most vividly for others, precisely those patterns or fragments of them, which, as he developed, filled most completely his idiosyncratic ego needs. Thus the unconscious processes of identification or rejection, of secondary elaboration, of distortion, and of inversion are operative in cultural assimilation as well as in dreams, and these processes in themselves are factors in cultural change.[16]

The informant whose dreams are used here is far from an average Hopi,[17] but neither is there justifiable evidence for the assumption that he is an unique one. Precisely because his needs were greater than average in some ways, he is an active dreamer who uses culturally provided sanctions in his dreams to reinforce his ego. But as one examines a cell under a powerful microscope in order to see its structure more clearly, so, too, is it frequently useful to examine configurations of behavior in exaggerated form so that similar processes in less vivid presentations are not overlooked. For sixteen years this man has recorded for me every dream which he could remember. These now total 292, plus eighteen others which were contributed to the project by Titiev and Simmons. We find that one third of these 310 dreams use specific folklore characters or themes, many combining several of these, and all applied effectively to Sam's (pseudonym)[18] personal problems.

Anticipating the inevitable question "are these really

dreams?" we can only say that it is very difficult to make up a story which has the disconnected, illogical quality of a dream; in any case they are "projections" in response to his own mind's images as he writes them down. And while Sam tends to give "order and coherency"[19] in recording what he calls his "dream stories," they still have the unmistakable quality of fantasy. Moreover, in this attempt to fashion the dream experiences into a "dream story," he uses the process of association to the original core of the dream, which brings to the surface not only conflict situations, but further fantasy interpretations which are selected from the "cultural storehouse," and modified or elaborated so that they can deal more effectively with ego-damaging reality.

To illustrate: in seventy-three of these dreams a highly personalized guardian spirit appears; in fifty-one of the seventy-three, this spirit is recognized definitely in face-to-face conversations as Sam's personal guide, who once took him safely to the land of the dead;[20] and in the other twenty-two the guide appears as various creatures—all of which also appear in Hopi tales—usually changing into human form for the purpose of encouraging or helping the dreamer in fear-provoking situations. Benedict has pointed out that although the Pueblo area is surrounded by the concept of a power-giving or protecting Guardian Spirit, such a concept has not been standardized in the Pueblo groups because they are dominated by the "necessity of the group ceremonial approach, not that of individual experience."[21] But in Sam we find a man who, because of various personal problems, although believing firmly in the "group approach," was frequently made to feel less a part of the community than he needed to feel. Consequently he has elaborated the concept of *dumalaitaka* (guide or guardian spirit), which is found among the Hopi, but which is generally rather vague and unstressed, into an ever present and active spirit who comes to him in dreams, takes him to witches' meetings and on treasure hunts, gives him strength, wisdom, and advice, rescues him from dangerous situations, and always assures him that he is on the right road and that his enemies are wrong. His comments indicate that he normally feels encouraged and happier after these dreams, in spite of the fact that many of them are night-mares from which he awakes sweating and sometimes crying.[22]

Titiev, puzzled by what he refers to as Sam's "almost unique" allusions to this spirit—both in dreams and conver-sations—questioned others about it, but found that Sam was the only man among them who made "constant and impor-tant references to it."[23] We have made a similar survey on both Second and Third Mesas with the same result.

Sam's dreams and associations to them are long and de-tailed, and neither space nor the purpose of this paper permit the inclusion or discussion of an entire dream as he recorded it. However, the following summaries are representative of the seventy-three dreams in which he receives security rein-forcement from his guide with regard to specific problems in his life.

A spirit wearing a hat like the War Twins runs ahead of the dreamer to Loloma Spring. His Guide appears, instructs him to catch the spirit, helps the dreamer (who frequently says that he is a poor runner) to run with great speed and thus to catch the spirit, who turns into the Water Serpent, goes into the spring, and promises plenty of rain and good crops. This, the dreamer says, is a *very* good dream.

The dreamer, also a poor hunter, dreams of hunting rabbits which change into naked, crying babies as he raises his gun to shoot. The Guide appears and gives him small pills with which to feed the babies. Later an old man at his home village tells him that he is a good man because he fed all of these babies, and that he will now have another baby of his own. [The informant had only five babies, a small number among the Hopi, and he had lost all of them. In addition to the in-supportable personal loss, this fact among the Hopi brings accusations of a bad heart, even witchcraft.]

In despair over the death of his adopted son, the dreamer is told by his Guide that he must "confess"[24] his bad thoughts; they hold a long conversation in which the Guide both scolds and comforts the dreamer, but emphasizes the fact that he is never absent from him.

Impotence, an even more destructive experience among the Hopi than among ourselves, cursed this informant for a time. In a dream which describes a *bahana* house, three fair girls are ordered by an old man to bathe before they receive the dreamer—a reversal of an actual humiliating experience with a white prostitute some thirty years before this dream. Later the old man says to the hesitating dreamer, "Don't be afraid— nothing will hinder you." Still hesitating, the dreamer is commanded by his Guide, appearing suddenly, to obey the old man. Eventually the girls turn into ears of corn and the informant realizes that in obeying instructions he has had a magical experience which will bring good crops to his people.

Of equal interest in indicating how myth is utilized in this informant's daily life are twenty-two dreams in which he has very personal experience with Palulukon, the Water Serpent, and eleven with Tuwapongwuhti, the Mother of all Wild Game. Summarizing from Parsons, the Water Serpent is, among other things, a punitive spirit among the Pueblos who sends earthquakes, landslides, and floods, particularly as punishment for sexual misconduct. She also notes that the Water Serpent Ceremony is a fertility ritual but says that curing is also indicated, possibly for venereal disease for men.[25] In Hopi myths[26] this serpent behaves generally as indicated above, objects to gossip and quarreling, and impregnates careless girls, but may be placated by the Hopi "Good Heart" and, if provided with a generous supply of prayer feathers, will give in turn—as fertilizing fluid[27]—an ample supply of water for the crops. Although there is an elaborate Palulukon ceremony in which, as Titiev says, both paraphernalia and procedure suggest a relationship between these powerful deities and other Hopi beliefs and ceremonies,[28] such relationships are obscured on both the personal and ritual levels by Hopi reluctance to discuss such fearful creatures.

But in his fantasy life at least, our dreamer has tamed Palulukon, and there follows, part in summary and part in his exact words, one of the nine dream encounters Sam has had with a Water Serpent.

The dreamer becomes aware that a woman's dance, Oaqöl, is in progress in the plaza. He is disturbed because such a dance at this time of year can ruin the crops. Invited to join the people in the plaza, he refuses and wanders off to rest under a tree. People pass, stare curiously, and whisper to each other about him. At last an old man tells him to get up and look behind him, saying, "There is something that we are afraid of." Sam replies, "There is nothing in this world that I fear of," but he gets up.

In his own words again, "There I saw a huge snake coil up. His head must be the size of the mountain lion and around the neck I saw four *pahos* (prayer feathers) hanging down. It seems to me that [it] is a sacred snake. 'Lay down,' said a voice. 'Sir, is that you speaking, Snake?' 'Yes, I am not going to harm you. You must obey me.' I lay down again in the shade and didn't pay any attention to that snake. Well the snake stuck his tongue out and began licking my face and hands. At first I [was] kind of scared, but remember that the snake would not harm me.

"Soon the snake put his body over my belly button and was very still. The snake must be around four hundred pounds. Well the snake began to move up to my head and put his nose close to my mouth, but I have to stand it. I remember he is not going to harm me. Well by and by X—— came along, and he must have seen that huge snake over my body. He ran to me and took a stick and try to chase that snake away, but the snake is too quick for him. He bound X—— round and round and was ready to crush him, but instead of kill X——, he sank down into the earth. I get up quickly and look down in the hole where the snake sank down into. I can see the movement of the water, a wave, like a boiling water. I notice the ground is shaking and the wind coming up. Everybody who have seen the snake take X—— down into the hole, they get after me. Some are crying. Then the people are running away in order to get away from me." [Among the associations to this dream we find the statement that X—— is the son of an important Oaqöl woman and: "she must love X——, so the snake show her how I feel when she accuse me of killing my babies (by witchcraft); she must be in that dance and the snake show her (that) her prayers are all wrong."]

"Well I left that hole and went into my house for I wanted to be with my wife and see if the world has come to end. I woke up and find that it is windy."

The above dream illustrates how in the Palulukon series also, personal themes of importance in the dreamer's life—

this time of bravery, moral superiority, revenge, and strongly implied sexual complications, among others—combine in dreams built around Hopi myth.

Tuwapongwuhti, whom he has sometimes actually "seen" far away in lonely spots, has also visited Sam in his dreams eleven times. She is the mother of all living things,[29] but is associated particularly with the wild game. There is a widespread belief that she may grant babies, that she gives game to hunters, and that she sometimes comes to men in dreams, occasionally desiring sexual favors. However, as with the Guardian Spirit and Palulukon, our survey failed to establish her as an important figure in individual psychology, although she more nearly approximates it than do these others. In her visits to Sam she sometimes comes as a "fierce ghost" eventually changing into a "beautiful maiden," or else reverses the procedure. In either case he resists her, becomes paralyzed with fear, and is eventually released, but she usually promises him the reward of game in exchange for *pahos* in spite of the fact that she has been denied his favors.

In considering this series of dreams, of which the following summary is typical, we must remember that our dreamer lost all of his children, and that he is a poor hunter. These are serious handicaps in Hopi society, in addition to the personal grief over losing one's children, and the personal inconvenience of being deprived of game food in a country where meat is a luxury.

The dreamer is hunting with *bahanas* and Hopis, but suddenly finds himself with just one spirit companion who eventually proves himself to be a witch. However, practicing the Hopi doctrine of being polite to witches, Sam continues with his partner. They talk all night, make *pahos* for Tuwapongwuhti and the game. The next day Sam is afraid of being shot by other hunters, is unlucky all day, but finally shoots a large deer. He calls for his companion to help him lift it.

Later, leaving camp he says, "I don't know why I go out there. But I was standing right by the tree and saw a fire coming up. It disappear into a valley and then come up again and change. It was a human shape coming at me. His light come out very bright and when he come near me he stopped and I watch him. It was that lady who owned the deer and rabbit, Tuwapongwuhti. She said, 'Now I'm looking for you. These twin fawns[30] that were born to me are your sons.'" Sam, astonished, asks how that can be, and is told that he made her pregnant by urinating on a certain spot of grass the night before. Quoting again, "This frighten me for I never think I do that, but anyway the two fawns are given to me and I took them, making my few steps back to camp, but she call me back. I turn back and saw that the Mother of these fawns change herself into a most beautiful young woman. She said, 'My husband, do not fear me. I'm your lovely wife.' With that she pull me close to her and she hold me tight. I woke up and found my wife putting her arm over my chest."

In addition to the ninety-three dreams mentioned above, folklore themes, such as visits to the home of the Parrots— who turn into human beings and back again—single dreams in which Spider Woman or Masau'u or others appear, make up a total of 117 out of the 310 dreams recorded by this man which are directly related to folklore. And this does not include many which quite probably relate to it, but which are not yet identifiable with any specific characters or tales examined by the writer to date.

Clearly, then, there is an interaction between Sam's dreams and Hopi folklore. He not only uses folklore in dreams but his dreams in turn modify the way in which he interprets folklore situations. By manipulating the problem solving[31] quality both of myths and his dreams, his fantasies not only give a sense of reality to his desire to be wise, strong, courageous, a good runner, and a good hunter who is honored by his people, and pleasing to and protected by supernaturals; but he is also frequently able through fantasy to operate within the cultural stock of imaginative happenings—elaborated or distorted to be sure—but still familiar enough to give him a *reassuring sense of identity with his people, even when rejected by them.* (In fact, it seems probable that a universal human need for "collective identity" rather than "limited imagination" is at work in the repetitive tendency noted in folklore.) We find, for instance, that in a tale reported by Titiev, Sitiyo, also, was a poor hunter, scorned by his kiva mates and afraid, but in exchange for his favors

Tuwapongwuhti, aided by Hawk, a mighty hunter, gave him many rabbits, and thus he won the respect of his fellows.[32]

This Hopi tale, like most of Sam's dream adventures, is contrary to daily experience, but in a culture where dreams are held to be important, and tales told by the old people as tribal history—usually in intimate situations of maximal group harmony—are the most satisfying part of one's education, both dreams and tales can be more rewarding than rational responses. After all life *is* hard, and among the Hopi, if one's heart is right, what has happened in the dim past *can* happen again! This illogical quality of wish fulfillment is evident at the manifest level in most of Sam's dreams, but his associations to specific dream statements (as to the hunting dream given above) reveal the repeated reassurance: "You may be like Sitiyo [or you may need help] but you are a good Hopi."

The materialization of fears in Sam's dreams was unfortunately real, but again, by fusing personal fears with similar ones which had plagued his culture's heroes, he was able to deal with anxiety in a somewhat impersonal manner so that it temporarily became less damaging to his ego and was partially eliminated. These heroes, too, needed—and received—supernatural support. Hallowell has shown how anxiety, socially directed, may have a positive social function.[33] Similarly, anxiety dreams, calling attention to one's infringement of the moral code, direct an individual toward conformity. But in addition, to the extent that they may be manipulated by the processes of identification, distortion or inversion *to give the dreamer a sense of unity with his culture, or freedom from group derogation,* they likewise play a positive role in individual psychology. In this connection we must remember that oral confession of the "bad thoughts" in a dream, which is Hopi custom—in itself an oblique admission of error—frequently leads in turn to the confession of questionable behavior and thus to the partial working out of tension-provoking guilt.

Moreover, both familiar tales and dreams elaborated into interesting stories attract an audience, one of the few socially approved ways of becoming the center of attention among the Hopi. Although it is a device which sometimes has unpleasant consequences, it is widely used by them, and is of particular importance to this dreamer, for while competitive creativity is frowned upon, one may relate—with questionable accuracy but usually with impunity—what the old uncles said, or may thoroughly exploit one's dream adventures. Here, as has been suggested above, an interaction between mythology and dreams becomes apparent, for the dreamer not only uses myths modified by his own psychology in his dreams, but to the extent that he relates his dreams convincingly, he introduces new emphases and directions into Hopi lore. In the dreamer's village, for instance, we have noted a gradually increasing interest in the possibility of a more active personal guide than the rather vague *dumalaitaka* whom they discussed with us a decade ago. The name remains the same, but in this village the spirit has become somewhat more real.

The results of the survey sketched above suggest that as anthropologists have often found it simpler to study cultural content and social organization in small and relatively homogeneous groups, rather than in large and diffuse ones, so, too, is it sometimes possible to examine the dynamics of segments of them—a kinship structure or a body of folklore—by studying intensively the way in which these shape individual lives. And in summary we again assert that while this dreamer is not a typical Hopi, neither can he be considered unique; we have reason to assume that both the individual and the cultural mechanisms which shape his dreams were at work in varying degrees and over various personal problems, among all Hopi, since these people share—in addition to the extracultural qualities which are innate in humanness—a remarkably integrated body of culture, in spite of factions and village splits. And while it is true that the relation between dreams and folklore is not so apparent in the three hundred dreams collected from other Hopi, it can be demonstrated to exist, particularly in those of the older and less acculturated people. For we find, as Herskovits has said, "In terms of a kind of socialized fantasy . . . folklore . . . shows itself a many-faceted vehicle of self-expression on both the conscious and unconscious level."[34]

NOTES

1. Stith Thompson, "Advances in Folklore Studies," *Anthropology Today,* ed. A. L. Kroeber (Chicago, 1953), p. 592.

2. Dreams cited in this paper are taken from a collection of Hopi dreams which was begun by the writer in 1939 in connection with an investigation of social and cultural change by F. Eggan.

3. See Werner Wolf, *The Dream—Mirror of Conscience* (New York, 1952), for a discussion of mythology and dreams. Also see William Morgan, "Navajo Dreams," *American Anthropologist,* XXXIV (1932), 390-406; and Jackson Steward Lincoln, *The Dream in Primitive Cultures* (Baltimore, 1934).

4. H. R. Voth, *The Traditions of the Hopi,* Field Columbian Museum, Anthropological Ser., VIII (Chicago, 1905).

5. Esther Goldfrank, "The Impact of Situation and Personality on Four Hopi Emergence Myths," *Southwestern Journal of Anthropology,* IV (1948).

6. See Leslie Spier, "Historical Interrelations of Culture Traits, Franz Boas' Study of Tsimshian Mythology," *Methods in the Social Sciences,* ed. Stuart Rice (Chicago, 1931).

7. Margaret Lantis, "Nunivak Eskimo Personality as Revealed in the Mythology," Anthropological Papers of the Univ. of Alaska, II, No. 1 (Fairbanks, 1953), 165-168.

8. Clyde Kluckhohn, "Myths and Rituals: a General Theory," *Harvard Theological Review,* XXXV, No. 2 (1942), especially 55-71. See also Dorothy Eggan, "The Manifest Content of Dreams: a Challenge to Social Science," *American Anthropologist,* LIV, No. 4 (1952), 471.

9. Jules Henry, "Culture, Education, and Communications Theory," *Education and Anthropology,* ed. George D. Spindler (Stanford, 1955).

10. Dorothy Eggan, "Instruction and Affect in Hopi Cultural Continuity" (MS., 1954).

11. B. L. Whorf, "The Relation of Habitual Thought and Behavior to Language," *Language, Culture, and Personality,* eds. L. Spier, A. I. Hallowell, S. Newman (Menasha, Wis., 1941), p. 92.

12. "The sense of *collective identity* is based on the convincing experience that the group's ways of synthesizing its existence at least at one time successfully integrated the economy of the individual life cycles and that of geographic-historial organization. The growing child derives a vitalizing sense of reality from the

awareness that his individual way of mastering experience (his ego-synthesis) is a successful variant of a group identity and is in accord with its space-time and life-span." Erik H. Erickson, "Childhood and Tradition in Two American Indian Tribes," *Personality in Nature, Society, and Culture,* eds. Clyde Kluckhohn and Henry A. Murray (New York, 1948), p. 198n.

13. In this connection Hallowell also calls attention to the way in which the belief system among the Saulteaux Indians compels an individual to see or interpret situations. A. I. Hallowell, "Aggression in Saulteaux Society," Kluckhohn and Murray, *Personality in Nature, Society, and Culture,* pp. 204-218.

14. M. J. Herskovits, *Man and His Works* (New York, 1950), p. 403.

15. Kluckhohn, "Myths and Rituals: a General Theory," 53.

16. Cf. Kluckhohn, "Myths and Rituals: a General Theory," 52.

17. David Aberle, in "Psychosocial Analysis of a Hopi Life History," Comparative Psychology Monographs, XXI, No. 1 (Berkeley and Los Angeles, 1951), points out that while no one person is typical, many of each person's problems are; see especially pp. 3 and 119.

18. Because of the very personal nature of the data discussed in this paper "Sam" has been substituted for the informant's real name.

19. Cf. W. J. Wallace, "The Dream in Mohave Life," *JAF,* LX (1947), 252-258. See also, Sigmund Freud, *New Introductory Lectures on Psychoanalysis* (New York, 1933), Ch. I.

20. For descriptions of such a Hopi visit to the land of the dead, see M. Titiev, "A Hopi Visit to the Afterworld," Papers of the Michigan Academy of Science, Arts, and Letters, XXVI (1940), 495-504; and L. Simmons, *Sun Chief, the Autobiography of a Hopi Indian* (New Haven, 1942), pp. 119-127, and Appendix, p. 435.

21. Ruth Benedict, *The Concept of the Guardian Spirit in North America,* Memoirs of the American Anthropological Assn., No. 29 (1923), p. 36.

22. Eggan, "The Manifest Content of Dreams," 482.

23. Mischa Titiev, personal communication.

24. Confession as a useful emotional purge is constantly recommended by the Hopi. They are instructed to wake someone, even in the middle of the night, to relate a bad dream, and they must then go outside and spit four times to rid themselves of evil thoughts. Cf. A. I. Hallowell, "The Social Functions of Anxiety in a Primitive Society," *Personal Character and Cultural Milieu,* ed. D. G. Haring (Syracuse, N. Y., 1948), pp. 375-389; and Weston

LaBarre, "Primitive Psychotherapy: Peyotism and Confession," *Journal of Abnormal and Social Psychology,* XLII, No. 3 (1947).

25. If, as Parsons suggests, curing for venereal diesase, as well as fertility, is one function of Palulukon rites, this fact also becomes important in considering Sam's Water Serpent dreams. See Elsie Clews Parsons, *Pueblo Indian Religion* (Chicago, 1939), pp. 184-186, 508.

26. Mischa Titiev, "Two Hopi Myths and Rites," *JAF,* LXI (1948), 31-43; W. Wallis, "Folk Tales from Shungopavi," *JAF,* XLIX (1936), 1-68; Walter Hough, *The Hopi Indians* (Cedar Rapids, Iowa, 1915); Voth, *The Traditions of the Hopi,* pp. 48-63.

27. H. K. Haeberlin, "The Idea of Fertilization in the Culture of the Pueblo Indians," Memoirs of the American Anthropological Assn., III, No. 1 (1916); see especially p. 23.

28. M. Titiev, *Old Oraibi,* Papers of the Peabody Museum of American Archaeology and Ethnology XXII, No. 1 (Cambridge, Mass., 1944), 121-124, 149.

29. A. M. Stephen, *Hopi Journal,* Columbia Univ. Contributions to Anthropology, XXIII (New York, 1936), 1313; M. Titiev, "Two Hopi Tales from Oraibi," Papers of the Michigan Acad., XXIX (1943), 431-437; Titiev, *Old Oraibi,* p. 137; Voth, *The Traditions of the Hopi,* 137-141; Simmons, *Sun Chief,* pp. 426-428.

30. For reasons too complicated for the space permitted in this paper, the dreamer is particularly interested in *antelope twins.*

31. Thomas French, *The Integration of Behavior,* Vol. I: *Basic Postulates* (Chicago, 1952), pp. 71-72.

32. Titiev, "Two Hopi Tales from Oraibi," pp. 431-437.

33. Hallowell, "The Social Functions of Anxiety," pp. 375-388.

34. Herskovits, *Man and His Works,* p. 421.

MYTH AND RITUAL

BY LORD RAGLAN

IT IS easy to refute the old-fashioned theories of myth, such
as that it is garbled history, or is the product of savage
speculation, but since the purpose of this paper is to explain
what a myth is, it is perhaps only necessary to say that in the
view of many modern students it is simply a narrative associated with a rite.

Let us take a simple example. In *Leviticus* X we are told
how Aaron performed a sacrifice: "his sons handed him the
blood, which he splashed on the altar all round . . . the fat he
burned on the altar." In Chapter XVII, in a later passage, we
are told that "the priest must splash the blood on the altar
. . . burning the fat as a soothing odour for the Eternal."

These are two descriptions of the same rite, but whereas
the latter is in the form of a simple instruction, the former is
a myth, that is to say an account of the rite told as a narrative of what somebody once did. It must have been written
down at a time when it was still thought necessary to validate
the rite by attributing its origin to an ancient and sacred
person, and this is what myths often do. The latter passage
must date from a time when the ritual had become so firmly

122

established that a simple instruction was all that was required.

Myths as a rule are untrue historically, because most
rituals have been developed gradually, and not as the result
of some historical incident; but this is not necessarily so.
Consider the pilgrimage to Canterbury, which resulted from
the murder of Becket. As the pilgrims performed the ritual of
touring the cathedral and singing hymns or praying at spots
connected with Becket's life and death, the story of these was
recited. This story, since it explained the ritual, could properly be described as a myth.

An interesting case is that of Guy Fawkes. The fifth of November was the date of an ancient fire festival, of which the
burning of a human victim must once have formed a part.
Fawkes was in fact hanged and not burnt, but his story has
nevertheless been adopted as the myth of this ritual.

We must make it clear, however, that myths, whether or
not they have any historical basis, may be of the highest religious importance, and for this purpose we turn to Hooke.
He says that "the story embodied in the myth of the slaying
of Tiamat is not historical in the strict sense. . . . But it possesses a truth which is both wider and deeper than the narrow truth of history. . . . The essential truth of the myth lies
in the fact that it embodies a situation of profound emotional
significance, a situation, moreover, which is in its nature recurrent, and which calls for the repetition of the ritual which
deals with the situation and satisfies the need evoked by it.
. . . It is in this sense that we may speak of the Christian myth,
without the slightest reflection on the historical character of
the events out of which the Christian religion sprang. The
term is used to express the fact of the ever-recurring repetition of a situation in which human need is met by the life-
giving potency of a sacral act."[1]

And James quotes Tennyson: "For wisdom dealt with
mortal powers, / Where truth is closest words shall fail,
/ And truth embodied in a tale / Shall enter in at lowly
doors." He says that the term *myth* may be applied in this
sense to the sacred story of Christian tradition, and so employed should give offense to none.[2]

According to Hooke, then, a myth with its associated ritual

is something which meets a recurrent human need, and we can safely say that this need is for life and prosperity in one form or another. This applies to every genuine myth. Even in so simple a myth as that of Guy Fawkes, the implication of "I see no reason why gunpowder treason should ever be forgot" is that if it were forgotten things might be easier for traitors. Hocart has shown that, in the case of the Hindu myths, "the myth itself confers, or helps to confer, the object of men's desire—life."[3] We can then extend our definition and say that myth is not merely a narrative associated with a rite, but a narrative which, with or without its associated rite, is believed to confer life.

But some readers may say that this is not at all what they mean by myths. What they mean are highly imaginative stories about the miraculous rescue of a princess from a monster, or the vengeance of the gods on a king who has incurred their wrath; how could such stories be supposed to confer life? Anyone who makes this objection has obviously limited his study of mythology to those myths which the classical writers abstracted from their religious context and used as a basis for poetry and romance. Myths in their proper context are seen differently, as will appear presently.

Those who regard myths as the products of the imagination have clearly not considered how the imagination works. Nobody can possibly imagine anything which has not been suggested to him by something which he has seen, heard, or read. Poets and novelists, by selecting from and combining ideas which have reached them in various ways, produce what are called works of the imagination, but those who formulated or recorded the myths could not have acted in this way. For the myths were so sacred that they could have been altered or added to only by those who believed themselves inspired, and even then to a very limited extent.

The kind of imagination which the myth-maker is, according to some, supposed to have possessed is in fact something which nobody has ever possessed. When Grote, for example, says that the ancient Greek, instead of seeing the sun as we see it, "saw the great god Helios, mounting his chariot in the morning in the east, reaching at midday the height of the solid heaven, and arriving in the evening at the western hori-

zon with horses fatigued and desirous of repose,"[4] he is postu-
lating a type of mind which has never existed. The chariot of
the sun was a ritual chariot, and the god Helios was seen in
the ritual in the form of a priest who drove the chariot. The
Christian believes that the consecrated wafer is the body of
Christ, but what he sees is a wafer. In the same way, we may
be sure, the ancient Greek believed that the sun was the god
Helios, but what he saw was just the sun.

It has often been suggested that there is a myth-making
stage through which all communities pass; but in that case all
but the most primitive communities would have a mythology
or traces of it, and if H. J. Rose is right that is not so. For he
assures us that the earlier Romans had no mythology, and
that the myths told of their gods by the later Roman writers
were borrowings from the Greeks.[5] The Romans had many
rites, but these were not associated with myths because the
gods were not fully personified, and without full personifica-
tion there can hardly be mythology. But if the Romans had no
mythology, how comes it that the Greeks, their neighbors
and kinsmen, had such an elaborate mythology? The reason,
unpopular with classical scholars but noted by many writers
from Herodotus to Sir Arthur Evans and Hooke, is that many
of the Greek myths were not native, but imported from
Egypt, Syria, and Mesopotamia. Herodotus, as is well known,
assigned an Egyptian origin to many elements in Greek religion and mythology; Hooke identifies Perseus with the
Canaanite god Resheph; and Evans traces the Minotaur to
the Euphrates. And in this connection Hooke notes that
"both the Minotaur and Perseus myths involve an underlying ritual pattern of human sacrifice, and take us back to
a stage in which the myth and ritual were united."[6]

Even those scholars who are in general hostile to the view
put forward in this paper have been driven to realize that in
some cases at least myth is linked with ritual. Thus H. J.
Rose, dealing with the mythical quarrel of Zeus and Hera,
and the Plataean rite which "commemorated" it, says that
"the legend has pretty certainly grown out of the rite, as
usually happens."[7] And Sir William Halliday says "that the
story of Lycaon, connected as it undoubtedly was with some
form of human sacrifice which seems to have persisted up

to the time of Pausanias, is an hieratic legend connected with the savage ritual of Lycaean Zeus, appears to me almost certain. The story of the serving up of Pelops by Tantalus may also have had a ritual origin and have been in the first place connected with some rite of human sacrifice and sacrament."[8]

A. B. Cook refers the legend of Ixion, who was bound to a wheel, to a ritual in which a man was bound to a wheel and sacrificed in the character of the sun-god, and the legend of Triptolemus, who was borne over the earth in a winged chariot from which he introduced the blessings of corn, to a rite of Eleusis. "The *protégé* of the goddess, mounting his winged seat, was swung aloft by means of a *geranos* or scenic crane."[9]

We end our quotations from the classical scholars with one from J. A. K. Thomson, who says: "Not only is the Myth the explanation of the rite, it is at the same time, in part at least, the explanation of the god. To primitive minds it is of such transcendent importance to get the ritual exactly right (for the slightest deviation will ruin everything) that the worshippers will not proceed one step without authority. And who is their authority? In normal circumstances the oldest man in the tribe, the worshipper who has been most frequently through this particular ceremony before. And his authority? Well, the oldest tribesman within his memory. And so the tradition goes back and back. . . . But it must end somewhere, and it ends, as a thousand instances show, in an imaginary divine founder of the rite, who becames the centre of the Myth."[10]

We may doubt whether the actual process was as Thomson suggests, but he correctly emphasizes the importance of the myth for the purpose of validating the rite. Hocart makes the same point when he writes: "If we turn to the living myth, that is the myth that is believed in, we find that it has no existence apart from the ritual. . . . Knowledge of the myth is essential to the ritual because it has to be recited at the ritual."[11]

Elsewhere, discussing Hindu mythology, he says that "we gradually come to realise that the sacrificer's object is to get control of the whole world—not temporal but ritual control;

that is, he seeks to bend the forces of nature to his will so that they may produce plenty for him. . . . As the gods did, so must the sacrificer, for the sacrificer and his acolytes represent the gods. It is necessary that he should know the myth which describes how the gods succeeded. . . . The myth is a precedent, but it is more than that. Knowledge is essential for the success of the ritual."[12]

Let us now turn to mythology as it is dealt with by students of the present-day savage, and begin with Malinowski. He says: "Myth, studied alive, is not symbolic but a direct expression of its subject-matter. . . . Myth fulfills in primitive culture an indispensable function; it expresses, enhances and codifies belief; it safeguards and enforces morality; it vouches for the efficiency and contains practical rules for the guidance of man."[13]

Malinowski's views have been amplified by Haimendorf in his account of the Raj Gonds, an Indian jungle tribe. He says: "The social norms regulating the tribal life of the Gonds are firmly rooted in mythology. They derive their validity from the ruling of culture-heroes and from the actions of deified ancestors recounted in epics and countless songs. The myths that tell of the origin of the Gond race and the establishment of the four phratries are more than history or folklore; they are the pragmatic sanction for institutions that determine the behaviour of every Gond towards his fellow-tribesmen, they are the vital forces inspiring the performance of the great clan feasts, and they define and authorise man's relations with the divine powers on whom his welfare depends. A relationship of mutual enlivenment links myth and ritual: as the myths lend power to the ritual acts, so the symbolic enactment of mythical occurrences during the cardinal rites of the clan feasts endows the myths with reality. . . . It is in the sacramental rites based on the clan-myth that the unity of the clan attains realisation."[14]

Of the Santals, a tribe of Northeastern India, Culshaw tells us that "many of the social activities of the Santals are based on myths, and the strength of their clan organisation is due in no small measure to its foundations in mythology. . . . When for any reason a piece of ritual associated with a myth falls into disuse, knowledge of the myth begins to die out;

conversely, when the myth is looked upon as outmoded, the activity with which it is linked begins to lose its hold on the people's imagination. . . . The decay of the ritual is leading to the disappearance of the ancient myth. It is nevertheless true that these stories do reveal the Santal view of the world. When they are told they call forth assent, and frequently in ordinary conversation the myths are cited in order to point a moral or clinch an argument."[15]

Among the Tallensi of the Gold Coast, so Fortes tells us, "the complementary functions of chiefship and *tendana*-ship are rooted directly in the social structure, but are also validated by myths of origin and backed by the most powerful religious sanctions of the ancestor cult and the cult of the earth."[16]

Other examples could be given, but these should suffice to show that myth and ritual are as closely linked among modern savages as they were in the ancient civilizations. Are we justified, however, in concluding that every rite has or once had its associated myth and every myth its associated rite? I do not suggest that this can be proved, but I do suggest that it can be shown to be probable.

Let us first consider rites which have no myths, as, according to Rose, those of the early Romans. Had they lost their myths, or had they never had any? The Roman rites were largely of the character which is commonly called magical. Frazer and his followers took the view that magic was, to put it shortly, primitive religion, and since many magical rites have no myth, this if true would prove ritual to be older than myths. But I have elsewhere given reason to think that Frazer was mistaken, and that magic, far from being primitive religion, is really degenerate religion, a form of religion, that is to say, in which people go on performing rites, but have forgotten why.[17] In Europe and, I believe, in America, many people perform such rites as "touching wood" after boasting, throwing three pinches of spilled salt over the left shoulder, saluting a magpie, turning money in their pockets when they see the new moon. They do not know why they perform them, except that failure to do so would be followed by "bad luck." It is difficult to believe that rites could have come into existence in such a vague and meaningless way, and it is probable that they were once associated with some deity or hero.

Evans-Pritchard spent some years in studying two tribes of the Southern Sudan, the Zande and the Nuer. Of the former he tells us that they have very few myths, and those he mentions have no close connection with the ritual.[18] The Nuer, on the other hand, have many myths. Some of these explain the mythological relationships of the lineages, and "also explain the ritual symbols and observances of the lineages mentioned in them."[19] It seems more likely that the Zande myths should have become lost or detached from the ritual than that the Nuer myths and rites should have originated independently and then been fitted together.

We come now to what is perhaps the more important and interesting question, whether every myth once had its associated rite. That many myths, ancient and modern, have been associated with rites we have seen, but are or were there myths which were never associated with rites? That there are now such myths is obvious, but my suggestion is that these myths were once associated with rites, and that the rites ceased to be performed but the myths survived in the form of stories. Having become divorced from their rites and recited for other purposes, they gradually changed their character. How this comes about is discussed by W. J. Gruffydd. Of one story in the *Mabinogion* he says that "the four stages through which the tale has grown to its present form can be set down as follows: 1st stage—Mythology. Of Lugh-Leu as a god we have considerable evidence. 2nd stage—Mythology becomes history. 3rd stage—Mythological history becomes folklore. 4th stage—Folklore is utilised to form literary tales."[20] A deity or ritual figure may, that is to say, become in succession a pseudo-historical character, a fairy prince, and the hero of a saga or novel, and unscientific mythologists will assign to each of these four personages a totally different origin. It seems legitimate, however, to regard as myths such narratives, whether quasi-historical or quasi-fictitious, as suggest a ritual origin, and we shall now consider some such myths.

Human sacrifice, real or symbolical, has been a prominent feature of most religions. Nobody has succeeded in explaining it, and I shall make no attempt to do so, but its evolution seems to have been in four main stages. In the first it was the divine king who was regularly sacrificed; in the second somebody else was regularly sacrificed as a substitute for the divine king; with the progress of civilization came a third stage, in which a human victim was sacrificed in times of emergency, but at other times a pretense was made of killing him, but some other victim was substituted. In the fourth stage the victim was never human, but was usually treated in such a way as to indicate that it once had been.

Many myths describe or refer to the sacrifice of a human victim. Some of them, those of Lycaon, Pelops, and Ixion, have already been mentioned. I wish now to draw attention to some myths which suggest the pretended killing of a human victim. The best known of these is of course that of Abraham and Isaac. What happened at one time, no doubt, was that a human victim was brought to the sacrificing priest, who made a pretense of killing him but instead killed a ram, which was substituted at the last moment. The myth, in the usual way, explains and justifies this procedure by reference to an ancient hero.

A story which has a wide distribution in Europe and Asia is that of the Faithful Hound, which in its simplest form is as follows: "The master's child is attacked by a wolf, but a hound which is guarding the child kills the wolf. The master on returning fails to see the child, but sees the hound covered with blood and believes that it has destroyed the child. He rashly kills the hound, but finds out his mistake when he discovers the child safe and the wolf killed. . . . It is generally agreed that this marchen is of Oriental origin."[21] I suggest that this was originally a myth describing and authorizing the substitution of an animal for a human victim.

The story of William Tell seems to have been told in many parts of Northern Europe long before it reached Switzerland,[22] and is probably a myth, that is to say the account of a pretended or substitute human sacrifice.

I have already mentioned the Minotaur. His death is depicted on many Greek vases, where we see a man with a bull's head being slain unresisting. He is said to have been the son of Queen Pasiphae, whom, incidentally, we know to have been a goddess worshipped in Laconia, by her intercourse with a bull. This does not suggest ritual until we compare it with the Vedic horse-sacrifice. Here, as so often, the wildest dreams of myth become the facts of ritual. A stallion was killed, the queen was made to lie beside it, and her next child was supposed to be its offspring. The king took part in this ritual, which most probably represents the substitution of a stallion for the king as victim. To be a ritually effective substitute the stallion had to be married to the queen. And at Athens the Queen Archon was married annually, in a building called the Ox-stall, to the bull-god Dionysus. (J. G. Frazer, *The Golden Bough,* VII [London, 1915] 30.) That these rites provide the clue to the myth of the Minotaur can scarcely be doubted.

Before considering myths which it is less easy to explain as narratives associated with ritual, we must discuss briefly two types of narrative which are not usually regarded as myths, the fairy tale and the saga. If we can show that these are, or were originally, associated with ritual, and can therefore on our definition be regarded as myths, we can avoid a good deal of hair-splitting. We can put all traditional narratives as regards their origin into one category, though it may be convenient to subdivide them according to the form which they have assumed.

Saintyves, in his study of Perrault's Tales, has given us good reason to think that such familiar stories as Bluebeard, Cinderella, Sleeping Beauty, and Little Red Ridinghood are associated with rites, either seasonal rites or rites of initiation. He starts with the story called "The Fairies." This story, variants of which are found in many countries, is of two sisters. One of them is kind to a fairy disguised as an old woman, and gives her food and drink; as a reward a jewel falls from her mouth whenever she speaks, and she marries a prince. The other sister is rude to the old woman and refuses to give her anything; as a punishment a frog falls from her mouth whenever she speaks, and she dies in misery. Saintyves shows that this story illustrates a ritual still performed in remote parts of France. On New Year's Eve the women of the household prepare a room, with a table on which are a clean tablecloth, food, drink, and a lighted candle. The door and window are left open for the fairies to come in. Those who are punctilious in this will be prosperous throughout the year and if unmarried will make a successful marriage; those who are neglectful will meet with dire misfortunes.[23]

This must suffice for the fairies, and we now turn to the sagas. It was formerly supposed that these were historical narratives, but it is now coming to be generally realized that they are novels based largely on myth. Danielli has found a pattern in many of the sagas, which briefly is as follows: The hero in youth is exiled and goes to the court of a king or chief, where he is insulted and treated with contempt. After some time a band of twelve berserks (which may mean "bear-men") arrives under the leadership of one called Bjorn (Bear). These put the hero through various ordeals, and challenge him to fight one of them; he does so and is victorious. After this he successfully undertakes to kill a great bear or other monster which has been ravaging the neighborhood. He is then taken into favor by the chief, and is given a valuable sword and in some instances the chief's daughter in marriage. The details vary, but there is enough regularity to leave little room for doubt that these are features of an installation ritual which have been adapted by the sagamen to their purpose of telling a good story.[24] In my book, *The Hero,* I have noted a number of other ritual features in the sagas.[25]

The rites to which I refer are known to have existed, so that we may safely infer that the stories told in the sagas, in whatever form they reached the sagamen, were once genuine myths. There are, however, many stories in myth form which are not known to have had associated rites; are we justified in assuming that such rites once existed? It is useless to discuss such questions in the abstract; let us take an example. Malinowski tells the Trobriand story of the origin of death. In the olden days people did not die when they grew old, but were able to rejuvenate themselves by taking off their skins. They lost this power because once a girl failed to recognize her rejuvenated grandmother, and the latter in pique put her old skin on again.[26] This story is not an explanation; the

Trobrianders, as Malinowski tells us, take no interest in explanations, and it obviously does not explain the fact of death. I suggest that it is a reminiscence of a new year ritual in the course of which an officiant, by taking off an old garment and putting on a new one, symbolically rejuvenated the world. I know of no such rite, but it may safely be postulated as the prototype of the many rites in which a change of dress symbolizes beginning of a new life.

In the foregoing I have drawn my evidence from books readily accessible to me, which unfortunately include few American ones. A cursory survey of American literature suggests, however, that in America as elsewhere many ethnologists have no idea that myths may have a function, and tell them as so many "Just So Stories." I have found some exceptions. Thus Parsons, discussing the Hopi "emergence" myth, says "this myth is too explanatory of the ceremonial life to be told to rank outsiders."[27] Wheelwright says of the Navaho: "in the most complete versions of the myths the different forms of ceremonies are mentioned and often described."[28] And Park, dealing with certain tribes of Colombia, says that the songs and dances conferred on the priests are among the themes which stand out in the myths.[29]

In conclusion, I would ask what are the objections to the view which I have put forward. There are few students of mythology, I suppose, who would deny that there is in some cases a connection between myth and ritual, but there is what seems to me a surprising reluctance to accept the simple scientific principle that similar causes produce similar effects, and a belief that a wide range of causes, from the wildest speculation to the soberest regard for historical truth, may produce stories sufficiently similar to be classed together as myths. To explain this phenomenon some theorists invoke a mysterious force called convergence, which is apparently supposed to get hold of all kinds of different things and force them into the same mold. But it is divergence, rather than convergence, which obtains in matters of culture; hence the variety of sects and dialects, and of objects in our museums. Myths are similar because they arise in connection with similar rites. Ritual has been, at most times and for most people, the most important thing in the world. From it have come music, dancing, painting, and sculpture. All these, we have every reason to believe, were sacred long before they were secular, and the same applies to storytelling.

NOTES

1. *The Labyrinth,* ed. S. H. Hooke (London, 1935), p. ix.

2. E. O. James, *Christian Myth and Ritual* (London, 1933), p. viii.

3. A. M. Hocart, *The Life-giving Myth* (London, 1952), p. 16.

4. Quoted by A. M. Hocart, *Social Origins* (London, 1954), p. 5.

5. H. J. Rose, *Primitive Culture in Italy* (London, 1926), p. 43.

6. *Myth and Ritual,* ed. E. H. Hooke (London, 1933), pp. 2, 6.

7. H. J. Rose, *A Handbook of Greek Mythology* (London, 1933), p. 104.

8. W. R. Halliday, *Indo-European Folktales and Greek Legend* (Cambridge, 1933), p. 103.

9. A. B. Cook, *Zeus,* I (Cambridge, 1925), 211, 218.

10. J. A. K. Thomson, *Studies in the Odyssey* (Oxford, 1914), p. 54.

11. A. M. Hocart, *The Progress of Man* (London, 1933), p. 223.

12. Hocart, *The Life-giving Myth,* p. 13.

13. B. Malinowski, *Myth in Primitive Psychology* (London, 1926), p. 13.

14. C. von F. Haimendorf, *The Raj Gonds* (London, 1948), p. 99.

15. W. J. Culshaw, *Tribal Heritage* (London, 1949), p. 64.

16. M. Fortes, *The Web of Kinship Among the Tallensi* (Oxford, 1949), p. 3.

17. Lord Raglan, *The Origins of Religion* (London, 1949).

18. E. E. Evans-Pritchard, *Witchcraft among the Azande* (Oxford, 1937), p. 442.

19. E. E. Evans-Pritchard, *The Nuer* (Oxford, 1940), p. 442.

20. W. J. Gruffydd, *Math vab Mathonwy* (Cardiff, 1928), p. 81.

21. W. J. Gruffydd, *Rhiannon* (Cardiff, 1953), p. 59; cf. S. Baring-Gould, *Curious Myths of the Middle Ages* (London, 1892), p. 134.

22. Baring-Gould, *Curious Myths,* p. 119.

23. P. Saintyves, *Les contes de Perrault et les récits parallèles* (Paris, 1923), p. 13.

24. Mary Danielli, "Initiation Ceremonial From Norse Literature," *Folk-Lore,* LVI (1945), 229-245.

25. Lord Raglan, *The Hero* (London, 1936), pp. 256, 264, 272, 278.

26. Malinowski, *Myth in Primitive Psychology*, pp. 41, 81.

27. E. C. Parsons, *Pueblo Indian Religion*, I (Chicago, 1939), 216.

28. M. C. Wheelwright, *Navaho Creation Myth* (Santa Fe, 1942), p. 19.

29. W. Z. Park, *Handbook of South American Indians*, II (Washington, 1946), 886.

THE RITUAL VIEW OF
MYTH AND THE MYTHIC

BY STANLEY EDGAR HYMAN

T HE ritual approach comes directly out of Darwin, and thus, I suppose, ultimately from Heraclitus, whose *panta rei* seems to be the ancestor of any dynamic account of anything. When Darwin concluded *The Origin of Species* (1859) with a call for evolutionary treatment in the sciences of man, he opened the door to a variety of genetic studies of culture, and when he showed in *The Descent of Man* (1871) that human evolution was insignificant organically although vastly speeded up culturally (we might not be so quick to say "ethically" as he was), he made cultural studies the legitimate heirs of evolutionary biology. The same year as *The Descent,* in response to *The Origin,* E. B. Tylor's *Primitive Culture* appeared, drawing an immediate fan letter from Darwin. It staked off quite a broad claim to cultural studies in its subtitle "Researches into the Development of Mythology, Philosophy, Religion, Language, Art, and Custom." Tylor's general principle, almost his law, is that survivals are significant because they embody, sometimes in trivial or playful form, the serious usages of earlier stages. In material culture, it meant that such important tools as the

bow and arrow, the fire drill, and the magician's rattle
evolved into the toys of children; in non-material culture, it
meant that myths were based on rites, although, like many
rationalists before him, Tylor believed that they had been
consciously devised as explanations.

Tylor's evolutionary anthropology, carried on by such suc-
cessors as R. R. Marett and Henry Balfour, became the central tradition of British anthropology, but the emphasis gradually shifted from Tylor's concern with belief and custom to
the more tangible areas of social organization, economics,
and material culture. Meanwhile, at Cambridge, a classicist
named James G. Frazer had found *Primitive Culture* a revelation, and his interest in ancient survivals was broadened
and extended by his friend William Robertson Smith's
studies of religion, in which Smith made use of the comparative method, invented by Montesquieu and developed by
German philology. Weaving together the two main strands
of Tylor's evolutionary survivals and Smith's comparative
method, in 1885 Frazer began publishing a series of periodical
articles on custom. When one of them, on a curious priesthood
at Nemi in Italy, tied in with Smith's ideas about the slain
god and outgrew article size, he kept working on it and in
1890 published it as the first edition of *The Golden Bough* in
two volumes, dedicated to Smith. For Frazer in *The Golden
Bough,* myth is still Tylor's rationalist "a fiction devised to
explain an old custom, of which the real meaning and origin
had been forgotten,"[1] and the evolution of custom is still
Tylor's "to dwindle from solemn ritual into mere pageant
and pastime,"[2] but Frazer constantly approaches, without
ever quite stating, a synthesis of the two, with myths not con-
sciously-devised rational explanations, but the actual
dwindling or later form of the rite. Long before 1915, when
the third and final edition of *The Golden Bough* appeared,
that synthesis had been arrived at.

Since 1882, Jane Ellen Harrison, Frazer's contemporary at
Cambridge, had been writing on Greek mythology and art,
and in 1903, after she had seen a clay seal at Cnossos with its
sudden revelation that the Minotaur was the king of Crete
in a bull mask, she published *Prolegomena to the Study of
Greek Religion,* which clearly stated the priority of ritual

over myth or theology. Her book acknowledged the cooperation of Gilbert Murray at Tylor's Oxford, and Frazer, F. M.
Cornford, and A. B. Cook at Cambridge. Cook, whose book
Zeus, did not begin to appear for another decade, began
publishing parts of it in periodicals about that time, and his
important series "Zeus, Jupiter, and the Oak" in the *Classical
Review* (1903) took an approach similar to Harrison's. By
the time Murray published *The Rise of the Greek Epic*
(1907), reading such mythic figures as Helen and Achilles as
ritual concretizations, he was able to draw on some of this
Cambridge work his earlier writings had influenced. By 1908,
when the Committee for Anthropology at Oxford sponsored
six lectures, published under Marett's editorship later that
year as *Anthropology and the Classics*, with the aim of interesting students of the humanities in "the lower culture,"[3]
students of the humanities at the sister university had been
turning their attention to the lower cultures for two decades,
and the seed Tylor planted had flowered elsewhere.

The watershed year was 1912, when Harrison published
Themis, a full and brilliant exposition of the chthonic origins
of Greek mythology, including an excursus on the ritual
forms underlying Greek tragedy by Murray (to whom the
book is dedicated), a chapter on the ritual origin of the
Olympic Games by Cornford, and copious material from
Cook's forthcoming work. (Curiously, this book too had been
inspired by a visit to Crete, where Harrison encountered the
"Hymn of the Kouretes," which suggested that ritual magic,
specifically the rite of a year-daimon, was the central element in early Greek religion.) In *Themis*, Harrison made
three important points with great clarity: that myth arises
out of rite, rather than the reverse;[4] that it is "the spoken
correlative of the acted rite, the thing done; it is *to legomenon*
as contrasted with or rather as related to *to dromenon*"[5] (a
Greek definition of myth is *ta legomena epi tois dromenois*
'the things said over a ritual act'); and that it is not anything
else nor of any other origin.[6]

Basic to this view, as Harrison makes clear, is a dynamic
or evolutionary conception of process whereby rites die out,
and myths continue in religion, literature, art, and various

symbolic forms with increased misunderstanding of the ancient rite, and a compensatory transformation for intelligibility in new terms. Thus myths are never the record of historical events or people, but freed from their ritual origins they may attach to historical events or people (as Alexander was believed to be, or claimed to be, a god and the son of a snake, because mythic Greek kings like Cecrops had been ritual snake gods); they never originate as scientific or aetiological explanations of nature, but freed from their ritual origins may be so used (as stars have their positions in the sky because the mythic hero threw them there, but *his* origin is in rite, not primitive astronomy).

The ritual approach to mythology, or any form based on myth, thus cannot limit itself to genetic considerations. In the artificial division I have found most handy, it must deal with the three related problems of Origin, Structure, and Function. If the origin is the ancient anonymous collective one of ritual, the structure is intrinsically dramatic, the *dromenon* or thing done, but that form ceaselessly evolves in time in the chain of folk transmission. Here the considerations are not historic nor anthropological, but formal in terms of literary structure, principles of *Gestalt* organization, and dynamic criteria. In folk transmission, the "folk work" involves operations comparable to those Freud found in the "dream work"—splitting, displacement, multiplication, projection, rationalization, secondary elaboration, and interpretation—as well as such more characteristically aesthetic dynamics as Kenneth Burke's principle of "completion" or the fulfillment of expectations, in the work as well as in the audience. In regard to function, as the myth or text alters, there is at once a changing social function, as the work satisfies varying specific needs in the society along Malinowskian lines, and an unchanging, built-in function best described by Aristotle's *Poetics* and Freudian psychology, carrying with it its own context, taking us through its structural rites. In other words, the book of Jonah in the reading satisfies our need to be reborn in the belly of the great fish as efficiently as the initiatory rites from which it presumably derived satisfied the same need in the initiates. If these are now as then "fantasy gratifications," they are the charismatic experiences of great art now, as they were the charismatic experiences of organic religion then.

In a relatively short time, the ritual approach to folk study has met with remarkable success. There had of course been individual ritual studies in various areas long before 1912. Most of them were in the field of children's lore, where ritual survivals, after Tylor had called attention to them, were readily apparent. Some of the earliest studies were William Wells Newell's *Games and Songs of American Children* (1883), Henry Carrington Bolton's *The Counting-Out Rhymes of Children* (1888), Alice Gomme's *The Traditional Games Of England, Scotland and Ireland* (1894), and Lina Eckenstein's *Comparative Studies in Nursery Rhymes* (1906). Much of this work has never been superseded, and similarly, the most impressive ritual studies we have of the Bible appeared at the turn of the century: for the Old Testament, William Simpson's *The Jonah Legend* (1899), and for the New, John M. Robertson's series of books on the mythic Jesus, beginning with *Christianity and Mythology* (1900). All of these people seem to have operated in relative isolation, independently working through to conclusions about their own material without knowing what was going on in other areas or recognizing the general application of their conclusions.

With the appearance of *Themis,* a powerful general statement of the theory buttressed by a prodigy of scholarship in several complicated areas of Greek culture, a "Cambridge" or "ritual" approach became generally available. Within a few years, its application to Greek studies had been enormously widened: Cornford's *From Religion to Philosophy* (1912), traced the ritual origins of some basic philosophic ideas; Harrison's *Ancient Art and Ritual* (1913), turned her theory on Greek plastic and pictorial arts; Murray tested his ritual forms on one tragic dramatist in *Euripides and His Age* (1913), (both it and *Ancient Art and Ritual* as popularizations for the Home University Library); Cornford tested the same forms on Greek comedy in *The Origin of Attic Comedy*

(1914); and the first volume of Cook's enormous storehouse of ritual interpretation, *Zeus,* appeared (1914).

The first application of the theory outside Greek studies was Murray's 1914 Shakespeare Lecture, "Hamlet and Orestes,"[7] a brilliant comparative study in the common ritual origins of Shakespeare and Greek drama. 1920 saw the appearance of Jessie Weston's *From Ritual to Romance,* treating the Grail romances as the "misinterpreted" record of a fertility rite, and Bertha Phillpotts' *The Elder Edda and Ancient Scandinavian Drama,* tracing the ritual sources of Northern epic poetry. The next year Margaret Murray's *The Witch-Cult in Western Europe* appeared, claiming a real "Dianic cult," the survival of the old pagan religion, persecuted by Christianity as witchcraft, the book constituting the first substantial excursion of the theory into history. In 1923, the widening ripples took in fairy tales, in P. Saintyves' *Les Contes de Perrault et les Récits Parallèles;* folk drama, in R. J. E. Tiddy's editing *The Mummers Play;* and law, in H. Goitein's *Primitive Ordeal and Modern Law.* In 1927, A. M. Hocart's *Kingship* appeared, tracing a great variety of material to a basic royal initiatory ceremony, and in 1929 Scott Buchanan's *Poetry and Mathematics* (the first American work along these lines in the third of a century since Bolton) boldly proposed a treatment of experimental science in ritual terms, and imaginatively worked some of it out.

In the thirties, S. H. Hooke edited two important symposia, *Myth and Ritual* (1933) and *The Labyrinth* (1935), in which a number of prominent scholars studied the relationships of myth and ritual in the ancient Near East; Lord Raglan published *Jocasta's Crime,* a ritual theory of taboo (1933), and his enormously influential *The Hero* (1937), which broadly generalized the ritual origins of all myth, as against the historical; Enid Welsford investigated the sources of an archetypal figure in *The Fool* (1935); Allen, Halliday, and Sikes published their definitive edition of *The Homeric Hymns* (1936), extending previous considerations of Greek epic and dramatic poetry into sacred lyric; and in the late thirties William Troy began publishing his as yet uncollected

ritual studies of such writers as Lawrence, Mann, and Fitz-
gerald.

By the forties, old subjects could be gone back over with
greatly augmented information. George Thomson combined
a ritual and Marxist approach in *Aeschylus and Athens*
(1941) and *Studies in Ancient Greek 'Society* (the first volume of which appeared in 1949); Rhys Carpenter amplified
Murray's earlier treatment of Homer in *Folk Tale, Fiction
and Saga in the Homeric Epics* (1946); Lewis Spence brought
Newell, Bolton, and Lady Gomme somewhat up to date in
Myth and Ritual in Dance, Game, and Rhyme (1947); and
Hugh Ross Williamson expanded Margaret Murray's brief
account (in *The God of the Witches,* 1933) of the deaths of
Thomas à Becket and William Rufus as Dianic cult sacrifices
in *The Arrow and the Sword* (1947). Venturing into fresh
fields, Gertrude Rachel Levy in *The Gate of Horn* (1948),
traced some ritual sources of culture down from the stone
age, paying considerable attention to plastic and pictorial art;
and in 1949 there were two important literary applications:
Francis Fergusson's *The Idea of a Theater,* a reading of
modern drama in terms of the ritual patterns exemplified in
Sophocles' *Oedipus the King,* and John Speirs' "Sir Gawain
and the Green Knight," in *Scrutiny,* Winter 1949, the first of
an important series of ritual studies of medieval English
literature.

So far in the fifties half a dozen new territories have been
explored and to some extent colonized. Theodor H. Gaster's
Thespis (1950) generalized a ritual origin for the whole body
of Near East sacred literature; Gertrude Kurath's articles
on dance in the Funk and Wagnalls' *Dictionary of Folklore*
the same year embraced a body of primitive and folk dance
forms in the same approach; Cornford's luminous "A Ritual
Basis for Hesiod's *Theogony*" was published posthumously
in *The Unwritten Philosophy* (1950, although it had been
written in 1941); and C. L. Barber published an ambitious
exploration of Shakespeare in "The Saturnalian Pattern in
Shakespeare's Comedy" in *The Sewanee Review,* Autumn
1951. Since then we have had the publication of Levy's second volume, *The Sword from the Stone* (1953), a ritual
genesis of epic; Herbert Weisinger's *Tragedy and the Para-*

dox of the Fortunate Fall (1953), a similar treatment of tragedy; and Margaret Murray's third book on the Dianic cult, *The Divine King in England* (1954). In this listing I have made no attempt at completeness, confining it to those writers with whose work I am most familiar, and only one or two titles by each (Murray, Cornford, and Harrison have written about a dozen books each), but the breadth and variety of even this truncated list should make it obvious that the "Cambridge" view has gone far beyond the confines of Greek mythology, and that it is apparently here to stay.

Since the ritual approach to myth and literature does not claim to be a theory of ultimate significance, but a method of study in terms of specific significances, it can cohabit happily with a great many other approaches. If its anthropology has historically been Frazerian, the comparative generalization across many cultures, many of its most successful works, from *Themis* to Speirs on Gawain, have stayed narrowly within one area, and where it deals with social function, its anthropology is most profitably Malinowskian (if an unusually historical Malinowskian). The Boas tradition in American anthropology, with its bias against cross-cultural generalization and evolutionary theory, in favor of empirical cultural studies and known history, has often seemed inimical to the ritual approach at those key points. Many of the Boas rigidities, however, seem to have softened in the decade since his death: the new culture and personality anthropology from Ruth Benedict's *Patterns of Culture* (1934) to E. Adamson Hoebel's *The Law of Primitive Man* (1954) seems as cheerfully comparative as *The Golden Bough;* we are all neo-evolutionists once again; and *Primitive Heritage* (1953), Margaret Mead's anthology with Nicholas Calas, calls for "the restoration of wonder," and means, apparently, let us take Frazer and Crawley more seriously. If out of this comes a neo-Frazerian generalizing anthropology, based, not on dubious material wrenched out of its configuration, but on detailed and accurate field studies done with Boasian rigor, no one would welcome it more than the ritualists.

In regard to psychology, the ritual approach can draw

centrally on Freudian psychoanalysis, informed by new
knowledge and less circumscribed by ethnocentric patterns.
This requires modernization without the loss of Freud's
central vision, which is tragic where such rebels as Adler and
Jung and such revisionists as Fromm and Horney are cheery
faith-healers; unshrinking where they bowdlerize; stubbornly materialist where they are idealist and mystic; and
dynamic, concerned with process, where they are static and
concerned with one or another variety of timeless *élan vital*.
After we have brought the Frazerian anthropology of *Totem
and Taboo* up to date and restored Freud's "vision" of the
Primal Horde, in Burke's terms, to its place as "essence"
rather than "origin," the book remains our most useful and
seminal equation of primitive rite with neurotic behavior,
and thus the bridge to Burke's own "symbolic action," the
private, individual symbolic equivalent for the ancient collective ritual. In the form of "symbolic action," psychoanalytic theory gives us the other dimension of function, the
wish-fulfillment or fantasy gratification, and can thus answer
some of our questions about the origins of origins.

As Jung's work increasingly seems to move toward mystic
religion and away from analytic psychology, it appears to be
of increasingly little use to a comparative and genetic approach. Strong as Jungian psychology has been in insisting
on the universal archetypal identity of myth and symbol, its
explanation of this identity in terms of the collective unconscious and innate awareness militates directly against any
attempt to study the specific forms by which these traits are
carried and transmitted in the culture (as did Freud's own
"memory traces"). As Jung is used in the work of Maud
Bodkin[8] or Joseph Campbell, as a source of suggestive insights, it seems far more to our purposes, and we can readily
utilize Campbell's universal "great myth" or "monomyth," a
concept itself derived from Van Gennep's *rites de passage:*
"a separation from the world, a penetration to some source
of power, and a life-enhancing return."[9] We must first, however, put the Jungian myth back on its roots, either a specific
myth and text (literary study) or a specific culture and rite
(anthropology). The ritual approach is certainly compatible
with varieties of mysticism, as the conclusions of Weston's

From Ritual to Romance or Harrison's *Epilegomena to the Study of Greek Religion* (1921) make clear, and Harrison was herself strongly drawn to Jung as well as to Bergson. Despite their examples, and the opinions of even so impressive a ritual poet as William Butler Yeats, the job of mythic analysis would seem to require a basic rational materialism, and a constant pressure in the direction of science and scholarship, away from mysticism and the occult. Within these limits of naturalism, and on the frame of this central concern with ritual, all possible knowledge and all approaches to myth, from the most meticulous motif-classification to the most speculative reconstruction of an *ur*-text, can be useful, with pluralism certainly the desirable condition.

There are only two varieties of approach, I think, with which the ritual view cannot usefully coexist. One is the euhemerist, the idea that myths are based on historic persons or events. This theory has been driven back from rampart to rampart over the years, but it stubbornly holds to each new defensive position: if it is forced to give up a historic William Tell, it retreats to a historic Robin Hood; if the historic Orpheus even Harrison's *Prolegomena* accepted in 1903 seems no longer tenable, perhaps Moses is; if there was no Leda and no egg, could there not have been a real Helen? By now, in regard to the great myths, we know that none of these is possible, even at those key points the Trojan War and the figure of Jesus. With stories unquestionably made up about real people, whether fictions about Napoleon or Eleanor Roosevelt jokes, it becomes a simple matter of definition, and if the euhemerists of our various schools want to call those stories myths, they are welcome to them. We find it more useful to apply some other term, insofar as the distinction between myth and history is a real and a basic one.[10]

The other approach to mythology that seems to offer no point of juncture with the ritual view is the cognitionist idea that myths derive from a quest for knowledge. In its nineteenth century forms, the theories that myths were personifications of nature, or the weather, or the sun and moon, it seems substantially to have died out; in various insidious twentieth century forms, the theories that myths are designed to answer aetiological questions about how death came into the world or how the bunny got his little furry tail, or that taboo is primitive hygiene or primitive genetics, it is still pervasive. Again, all one can say is that myths do not originate in this fashion, that primitive peoples are speculative and proto-scientific, surely, but that the lore they transmit is another order of knowledge. If they knew that the tabooed food carried trichinoisis or that the tabooed incestuous marriage deteriorated the stock, they would not save the first for their sacred feasts and the second for their rulers. Once more, if our various cognitionists want to call myth what is unquestionably primitive proto-science, like techniques for keeping a pot from cracking in the firing or seasonal lore for planting and harvesting, that is their privilege. The Alaskan Eskimos who took the Russian explorers for cuttlefish "on account of the buttons on their clothes," as Frazer reports,[11] obviously had speculative minds and a sense of continuity between the animal and human orders not unlike that informing Darwin's theory, but the difference between their myth of "The Great Cuttlefish That Walks Like a Man" (if they had one) and *The Origin of Species* is nevertheless substantial.

If we keep clearly in mind that myth tells a story sanctioning a rite, it is obvious that it neither means nor explains anything; that it is not science but a form of independent experience, analogous to literature. The pursuit of cognition in myth or folk literature has led to all the worst excesses of speculative research, whether the political slogans and events Katherine Elwes Thomas found hermetically concealed in nursery rhymes in *The Real Personages of Mother Goose* (1930), the wisdom messages, deliberately coded and jumbled, that Robert Graves uncoded in *The White Goddess* (1948), or, most recently, the secret fire worship Flavia Anderson discovered hidden behind every myth in *The Ancient Secret* (1953).

Among the important problems facing the ritual view at present is an adequate working out of the relationship between ritual, the anonymous regular recurrence of an action, and history, the unique identifiable experience in time. The problem is raised dramatically in the latest book by Margaret Murray, one of the pioneers of ritual studies. Called *The Divine King in England,* it is the third in her series on the Dianic cult and easily her wildest. Where *The Witch-cult in Western Europe* named two historical figures, Joan of Arc and Gilles de Rais, as voluntary sacrificial figures in the cult, and her second book, *The God of the Witches,* added two more, Thomas à Becket and William Rufus, the new book makes the bold claim on English history that "at least once in every reign from William The Conqueror to James I the sacrifice of the Incarnate God was consummated either in the person of the king or in that of his substitute,"[12] generally in a regular seven-year cycle. Since I have already reviewed the book at length for a forthcoming issue of *Midwest Folklore,* I can here only briefly summarize the problem. Murray's historical excursion is not only dubious history (as reviewers have pointed out, showing the errors of dates and durations by which she gets her seven-year victims, the number jugglery by which she gets her covens of thirteen), it is totally unnecessary history. She is certainly right about survivals of the old religion into modern times, but she seems to be basically in error about the manner in which it survives, to be confusing origins with events. As the ancient rites die out in literal practice, their misunderstood and transformed record passes into myth and symbol, and that is the form in which they survive and color history, without being themselves the events of history. In English history, assuming as she does that the primitive divine king was once slain every seven years, the monarch and his subjects might very well feel an ominousness about each seventh anniversary, and might welcome the death of the king or some high personage, but the step from that to the idea that the dead man was therefore the voluntary victim of a sacrificial cult is the unwarranted one. Murray's witch cult was a genuine worship of the old gods, surviving into modern times in a distorted form, but her Royal Covens are only the travesty of historical scholarship.

If the fallacy of historicity is still with us, the fallacy of aetiology may finally be on its way out. In *Themis,* as far back as 1912, Harrison wrote:

The myth is not at first aetiological, it does not arise to give a reason; it is representative, another form of utterance, of expression. When the emotion that started the ritual has died down and the ritual though hallowed by tradition seems unmeaning, a reason is sought in the myth and it is regarded as aetiological.[13]

In his recent posthumous volume edited by Lord Raglan, *The Life-Giving Myth* (1952), A. M. Hocart finally shows the process whereby myth goes beyond explaining the ritual to explaining other phenomena in nature, thus functioning as general aetiology. In Fiji, he reports, the physical peculiarities of an island with only one small patch of fertile soil are explained by a myth telling how Mberewalaki, a culture hero, flew into a passion at the misbehavior of the people of the island and hurled all the soil he was bringing them in a heap, instead of laying it out properly. Hocart points out that the myth is used aetiologically to explain the nature of the island, but did not originate in that attempt. The adventures of Mberewalaki originated, like all mythology, in ritual performance, and most of the lore of Hocart's Fijian informants consisted of such ritual myths. When they get interested in the topography of the island or are asked about it, Hocart argues, they do precisely what we would do, which is ransack their lore for an answer. Our lore might include a body of geological process, and we would search through it for an explanation; theirs has no geology but tells the acts and passions of Mberewalaki, and they search through it similarly and come up with an explanation. It should take no more than this one pointed example, I think, to puncture that last survival of the cosmological origin theories, the aetiological myth, except as a category of function.

After the relationship to history and to science or cognition, we are left with the relationship of ritual theory to belief. For Harrison, as for Frazer, ritual studies were part of comparative religion, and a hoped-for result, if not the ultimate aim, was finding a pattern in which a person of sense or sensibility could believe. Harrison concludes her essay in the Darwin centenary volume: "It is, I venture to think, towards the apprehension of such mysteries, not by reason only, but by man's whole personality, that the religious spirit in the course of its evolution through ancient magic and modern mysticism is ever blindly yet persistently moving."[14] In the course of his researches, Darwin himself lost most of his faith, but for Asa Gray, as for some Darwinians since, the doctrine of evolution celebrated God's powers and strengthened Christian faith. For John M. Robertson, the demolition of the historicity of Jesus was a blow against Christianity on behalf of free-thought; for W. B. Smith and Arthur Drews it was a way of purifying Christianity by purging it of legendary accretions. William Simpson seems to have hit on the idea of Jonah as an initiation ritual because he was preoccupied with such matters as a Freemason. There is apparently no necessary correlation between knowledge and belief; to know all is to believe all, or some, or none.

Most contemporary ritual students of myth, I should imagine, are like myself unbelievers, and it would seem to get progressively more difficult to acknowledge the essential identity of religious myths, and their genesis from the act of worship itself, the god out of the machinery, while continuing to believe in the "truth" of any one of them (or of all of them, except in the woolliest and most Jungian fashion). On the other hand, in *Cults and Creeds in Graeco-Roman Egypt* (1953), we saw Sir Harold Idris Bell, a professional papyrologist, produce a learned and impressive study of the pragmatic competition of religions in Hellenistic Egypt, with the constant proviso that one of those systems, Christianity, was not only morally superior to the others, but was the divinely inspired true faith. So perhaps to know all *is* to believe all.

Finally, then, a number of technical problems remain. In its brief history, the ritual view has illuminated almost the whole of Greek culture, including religion, philosophy, art, many of the forms of literature, and much else. It has done the same for the games, songs, and rhymes of children; the Old and New Testaments, epic and romance, edda and saga, folk drama and dance, folktale and legend, Near East religion, modern drama and literature, even problems in history, law, and science. A few forms of folk literature have not yet been explored in ritual terms, prominent among them in the English and Scottish popular ballads (the present writer has made a tentative foray in that direction) [15] and the American Negro blues. A ritual origin for the ballads presumes a body of antecedent folk drama, from which they evolve as narrative songs (as it in turn derives from ritual sacrifice), which hardly exists except in a few late poor fragments such as Robin Hood plays, and which must consequently be conjectured. Such conjecture is not impossible, but it is a hard job involving heavy reliance on that frail reed analogy, and it still awaits its doer. The blues raise serious problems. If they are a true folksong of ancient anonymous collective ritual origin, rather than a folk-transmitted song of modern composition, then they precede any American conditions experienced by the Negro and must have an African source. No trouble here, except that nothing like them has ever been found in Africa, perhaps because it does not exist, perhaps because it would look so different before its sea change that no one has yet identified it. In any case, a ritual origin for the blues constitutes a fascinating problem, although not a critical issue (too much obviously convincing ritual interpretation has been produced for the theory to stand or fall on any single form). A ritual account of the ballads and the blues would close two large chinks, and might keep out drafts even in the coldest climate of opinion.

The relationship of ritual and ritual myth to formal literature has hardly yet been touched. The brilliant work that should have inaugurated such a movement in literary criticism was Murray's 1914 Shakespeare Lecture, "Hamlet and Orestes," in which he showed the essential identity of the two dramatic heroes, not as the result of any direct linkage between the two, but because Shakespeare's Hamlet, through a long Northern line of Amlethus, Amlodi, and Ambales, derived from precisely the same myth and rite of the Winter King—cold, mad, death-centered, bitter, and filthy—that Orestes derived from in his warmer clime. The plays are neither myth nor rite, Murray insists, they are literature, but myth and rite underlie their forms, their plots, and their characters. (Greek drama itself represents a fusion of two separate derivations from ritual: the forms of Attic tragedy arise out of the sacrificial rites of tauriform or aegliform Dionysos, the plots of Attic tragedy come mostly from

Homer; and the bloody plots fit the ritual form so well, as Rhys Carpenter showed most fully, because the Homeric stories themselves derive from similar sacrificial rites far from Mount Olympus.) In the four decades since Murray's lecture, literary criticism has scarcely noticed it. A student of Murray's, Janet Spens, published a ritual treatment of Shakespeare, *An Essay on Shakespeare's Relation to Tradition* (1916), which I have never seen, but which Barber describes with serious reservations, and until his own essay almost nothing had been done along that line. Troy and Fergusson have dealt with a handful of novels and plays in ritual terms, Carvel Collins has written several essays on Faulkner, and the present writer has similarly tackled Thoreau and a few others, but there has been very little else.

The chief difficulty seems to lie in the need to recognize the relationship of literature to folk tradition, while at the same time drawing Murray's sharp line between them. Literature is analogous to myth, we have to insist, but is not itself myth. There has been a great deal of confusion on this point, best exemplified by Richard Chase's *Quest for Myth and Herman Melville* (both in 1949). Chase simply equates the two, defining myth in the former as "the aesthetic activity of a man's mind,"[16] turning Melville's works in the latter into so many myths or mythic organizations. Here we ought to keep in mind a number of basic distinctions. Myth and literature are separate and independent entities, although myth can never be considered in isolation, and any specific written text of the protean myth, or even fixed oral text, can fairly be called folk literature. For literary purposes, all myths are not one, however much they may be one, the monomyth or ur-myth, in essence or origin. What such modern writers as Melville or Kafka create is not myth but an individual fantasy expressing a symbolic action, equivalent to and related to the myth's expression of a public rite. No one, not even Melville (let alone Moritz Jagendorf) can invent myths or write folk literature.

The writer can use traditional myths with varying degrees of consciousness (with Joyce and Mann perhaps most fully conscious in our time), and he often does so with no premeditated intention, working from symbolic equivalents in his own unconscious. Here other arts closer to origins, like the dance, where the ritual or symbolic action is physically mimed, can be profoundly instructive. Just as there are varying degrees of consciousness, so are there varying degrees of fruitfulness in these uses of traditional patterns, ranging from dishonest fakery at one extreme to some of the subtlest ironic and imaginative organizations in our poetry at the other. The aim of a ritual literary criticism would be the exploration of all these relations, along with missionary activity on behalf of some of the more fruitful ones.

What begins as a modest genetic theory for the origin of a few myths thus eventually comes to make rather large claims on the essential forms of the whole culture. If, as Schroedinger's *Nature and the Greeks* (1954) shows, the patterns of Greek myth and rite have been built into all our physics until the last few decades, perhaps ritual is a matter of some importance. Raglan and Hocart argue that the forms of social organization arise out of it, Goitein throws in the processes of law, Cornford and Buchanan add the forms of philosophic and scientific thinking (perhaps all our thinking follows the ritual pattern of *agon* or contest, *sparagmos* or tearing apart, then *anagnorisis* or discovery and *epiphany* or showing-forth of the new idea). Even language itself suggests at many points a ritual origin. From rites come the structures, even the plots and characters, of literature, the magical organizations of painting, the arousing and fulfilling of expectation in music, perhaps the common origin of all the arts. If ritual is to be a general theory of culture, however, our operations must get more tentative and precise in proportion as our claims become more grandiose. We then have to keep distinctions even clearer, know so much more, and use every scrap of fact or theory that can be used. Having begun so easily by explaining the myth of the Sphinx, we may yet, working humbly in cooperation with anyone who will and can cooperate, end by reading her difficult riddle.

NOTES

1. J. G. Frazer, *The Golden Bough,* IV (London, 1915), 153.
2. Frazer, *The Golden Bough,* IV, 214.

3. *Anthropology and the Classics,* ed. R. R. Marett (Oxford, 1907), p. 5.

4. J. E. Harrison, *Themis* (Cambridge, 1912), p. 13.

5. Harrison, *Themis,* p. 328.

6. Harrison, *Themis,* p. 331.

7. In Gilbert Murray, *The Classical Tradition in Poetry* (Cambridge, Mass., 1927), pp. 205-240.

8. Maud Bodkin, *Archetypal Patterns in Poetry* (London, 1934), and *Studies of Type-Images in Poetry, Religion, and Philosophy* (London, 1951).

9. Joseph Campbell, *The Hero with a Thousand Faces* (New York, 1949), pp. 10, 35.

10. Myth must also be distinguished from all the other things we loosely call by its name: legend, tale, fantasy, mass delusion, popular belief and illusion, and plain lie.

11. Frazer, "Some Primitive Theories of the Origin of Man," *Darwin and Modern Science,* ed. A. C. Seward (Cambridge, 1909), p. 159.

12. M. A. Murray, *The Divine King in England* (London, 1954), p. 13.

13. Harrison, *Themis,* p. 16.

14. Harrison, "The Influence of Darwinism on the Study of Religions," *Darwin and Modern Science,* ed. A. C. Seward, p. 511.

15. S. E. Hyman, "The Raggle-Taggle Ballads O," *The Western Review,* XV (1951), 305-313.

16. Richard Chase, *Quest for Myth* (Baton Rouge, La., 1949), p. vii.

THE SEMANTIC
APPROACH TO MYTH

BY PHILIP WHEELWRIGHT

As an initial definition of myth I am content to borrow the one recently published by Alan W. Watts: "Myth is to be defined as a complex of stories—some no doubt fact, and some fantasy—which, for various reasons, human beings regard as demonstrations of the inner meaning of the universe and of human life."[1] This definition has the negative advantage of avoiding any connotation of "untrue" or "unhistorical" as a necessary part of the meaning, and the positive advantages of stressing both the narrative character and the transcendent reference of myth. These two latter properties, however, need to be qualified with some care, lest they involve us in undue limitations of the myth concept.

Regarding the narrative aspect of myth, we may take our bearings by two rather extreme and contrary views. The one, represented by Cassirer, treats myth as primarily a matter of perspective, and in this vein Cassirer speaks of "transposing the Kantian principle"—that all knowledge involves, at the instant of its reception, a synthesizing activity of the mind—"into the key of myth."[2] Myth here becomes a synonym of the mythopoeic mode of consciousness—a view that is reflected or at least adumbrated, I should think, both in Lévy-Bruhl's theory of participation and in Susanne Langer's treatment of myth as a primary type of human expression, parallel to, but distinct from, those two other primary types, language and art.[3] At the opposite extreme from this view, which defines "myth" without any necessary implication of "narrative" (although recognizing that mythic envisagement may, in fact, have a strong tendency to develop into narrative forms), we may place the view, lately revived in Richard Chase's *Quest for Myth,* that "myth is literature and must be considered as an aesthetic creation of the human imagination";[4] in other words, that the earliest mythologizers were individual poets—or, by modern analogy, novelists—constructing out of their especially sensitive imaginations tall tales characterized by a peculiar complication "of brilliant excitement, of the terrific play of the forces natural and human," and eventuating in some deeply desired and socially sharable feeling of reconciliation among those forces.

In any such controversy as this, concerning what myth "is," there is danger of confusing questions of fact with questions of definition. While questions of fact are the terminally important ones, we can behold them steadily only if we first settle the question of definition on an accurately relevant basis. It is pretty obvious that Chase, who takes myth as a species of literature, and Langer, who follows Cassirer in distinguishing between myth and art as separate categories, are not working from the same initial definition. Without wishing to claim anything like finality in the matter I would offer, as a tentative classificatory principle, a threefold conception of myth; or (as it may be regarded) a theory of three main ways in which "myth" has been, and may legitimately be, conceived. For convenience I shall call them *primary* myth, *romantic* myth, and *consummatory* myth. Of course in any particular mythic instance we must be prepared to expect some overlapping.

Briefly (since I have not yet focused down to the main point of my paper) I would say that Cassirer and Langer are dealing with myth in the primary sense, as a basis, and even perhaps in some instances as a pre-linguistic tendency, of human envisagement; whereas Chase is taking myth in the romantic sense (as connoting *le roman,* or deliberately contrived story), although with rumblings of universality which never become quite explicit. (I hope it will be recognized that I intend nothing pejorative in reviving this now slightly soiled word "romantic".) The consummatory myth, as I conceive it, is a product of a somewhat late and sophisticated stage of cultural development: a post-romantic attempt to recapture the lost innocence of the primitive mythopoeic attitude by transcending the narrative, logical, and linguistic forms which romantic mythologizing accepts and utilizes. Admittedly the line between the romantic and the consummatory is wavering and obscure; nevertheless we can hardly deny a significant difference of tone, technique, and quality of insight as we pass from the bright epic-Olympian story-forms of Homer to the utilization of symbols and patterned imagery in Aeschylus and Pindar, or from the faery-fantasy of *A Midsummer Night's Dream* to Shakespeare's utilization in *The Tempest* of neo-Platonic symbols to throw open the vision of a brave new world of peculiar values and destinies, or from the straightforward storytelling of any typical nineteenth century novel (or its stunted descendant, the television drama) to such a charting of unknown seas as in Kafka's *The Castle.* Indeed, I tend to think that the idea of consummatory myth offers a clue to the mysteries of much modern art—perhaps even to what is most authentic in all modern art, of which Picasso's *Guernica,* with its agonized repudiation of hitherto acceptable forms of construction and its single-pointed insistence upon the reality of dislocation, enormity, and pain, might stand as an eminent representative.

My purpose in distinguishing these three meanings, or modes, or (it may be) stages of myth has been to separate out the first of them for clearer analysis. For myth in its primary aspect bears a special relationship to language, and the exploration of this relationship strikes me as a particularly useful way of discovering something about the nature of myth and language alike. Unfortunately, that towering nineteenth century scholar, Friedrich Max Müller, has muddied the waters of this particular stream by his too provocative remark that myth is a "disease" of language, and by the subsequent eddies of doubt as to whether his etymological examples were sufficiently representative. For even though disease may have its creative side—as the pearl in the oyster and the last quartets of the deaf Beethoven attest—the word implies a derogatory valuation which is quite arbitrary with respect to the evidence. Accordingly, I propose that we reconsider the basic relationship between primary myth and the linguistic function without the use of shock-tactics and relying more upon semantic analysis and the known meanings of certain mythic symbols than upon the sometimes risky hypotheses of philology.

To clarify the question before us I am obliged to repeat, in brief summary, a distinction which I have developed at some length elsewhere:[5] the distinction between *steno-language* (the language of plain sense and exact denotation) and *expressive language* (such as is found to varying degree in poetry, religion, myth, and the more heightened moments of prose and of daily conversation). These two complementary and interpenetrating uses of language are the outgrowth, by and large, of two complementary semantic needs: to designate clearly as a means to efficient and assured communication, and to express with maximum fullness. The two are not always in actual conflict, to be sure; for many of the everyday ideas that we need to communicate have only a limited *relevant* fullness. But the criteria of relevance are altered by context, circumstance, and intention, and there are occasions when a writer or speaker cannot avoid the chance of whether to put primary emphasis upon wide-scale communicability or upon associative fullness and depth.

Myth in its first phase, the primitive, generally arises in an age before steno-language has been evolved to any marked extent, and consequently when some kind of expressive language is still the widely current medium of linguistic encounter. Or it may be that certain characteristics of steno-language have been developed for secular, everyday practical use, whereas expressive language is employed in that wide area which may be designated "sacred," and which doubtless includes those forms of story-making that have enough transcendental reference to be properly classified as "myth." Conseqently, in order to estimate what effect language may have had upon the early growth and character of myth, it will be desirable to survey certain main characteristics of expressive language.

First, then, into what, if any, components can expressive language be analyzed for the sake of inspecting its modes of operation more minutely? In steno-language the basic elements are easy to identify: they are the *term*—which is non-assertorial: it simply means, but does not declare; and the *proposition*—which is an assertorial relation between terms. That is to say, a proposition ("The dog barks") can be meaningfully affirmed or denied, whereas a term ("dog") cannot. In expressive language, on the other hand, no such tidy distinction can be maintained. For terms and propositions, in their strict logical signification, are the products of a considerable logical and linguistic evolution, and their analogues in expressive language do not ordinarily show such clear-cut outlines and differences. Nevertheless, such analogues do exist even in the most fluid, exalted, and emotively charged language. A rough distinction can still be found between its non-assertible and its assertible or quasi-assertible elements; and for purpose of easy reference I shall call these elements by the names *diaphor* and *sentence* respectively.

By "diaphor" (a word coined by Friedrich Max Müller) I mean approximately what the term "metaphor" has come to mean in some contemporary writing, according to Herbert Read's definition of it as "the expression of a complex idea, not by analysis, not by direct statement, but by the sudden perception of an objective relation."[6] But since the older definition of metaphor, as "the transference (*epi-phora*) of a name from the thing which it properly denotes to some other thing,"[7] is still widely current, we can better avoid ambiguity by using the less familiar, more neutral term. *Meta-phora* connotes motion—i.e., what may be figuratively conceived as a semantic motion, or the production of meaning—away from the already settled meaning of a term to an unusual or contextually special meaning: as when a man of filthy habits is called a pig. But such metaphoric transfer is possible only where certain terms with already settled meanings are available as starting-points; it is, therefore, more characteristic of the romantic phase of myth than of the primitive. There is a prior semantic movement which operates, often pre-consciously, by bringing raw elements of experience—qualities, capabilities, emotionally charged suggestibilities, and whatever else—into the specious unity of being represented by a certain symbol. Such primitive meanings are formed by a kind of semantic "motion" (*phora*) through (*dia*) a number of experiential elements, related in the first instance, no doubt, by a sort of vague but highly charged and tribally infectious emotive congruity, and then gradually formalized into a tribal tradition. Such a semantic motion seems to be indicated, for instance, by the Sioux Chief Standing Bear's explanation of the multiple yet unified significance of the pipe for his people: "The pipe was a tangible, visible link that joined man to Wakan Tanka and every puff of smoke that ascended in prayer unfailingly reached His presence. With it faith was upheld, ceremony sanctified, and the being consecrated. All the meanings of moral duty, ethics, religious and spiritual conceptions were symbolized in the pipe. It signified brotherhood, peace, and the perfection of Wakan Tanka, and to the Lakota [Dakota?] the pipe stood for that which the Bible, Church, State, and Flag, all combined, represented in the mind of the white man."[8]

Of course any such catalogue of diaphoric meanings is a cutting of the cloth into retail lengths. In the mythopoeic mode of consciousness there is a strong tendency of the different experiential elements to blend and fuse in a non-logical way. And not only that, but the selfhood of the worshiper tends to blend with them; that is to say, he becomes a full participant, not a mere observer. Finally, there is a blending, or partial blending, of worshiper and sacred objects and ceremonial acts with certain transcendent Presences—such as, for the Sioux, the Four Winds and the great spirit Wakan Tanka.

The last of these dimensions of the participative law points to a most important aspect of much diaphoric language: namely, its concrete universality, or archetypal character. I would suggest (although I am not sure how far the generalization will carry) that the most forceful archetypes are likely to arise out of a diaphoric situation where as least two of the diaphorically related elements represent human functions or interests of a deep-going and pertinently associated sort. Thus to the ancient Egyptians the scarab, or dung-beetle, was a symbol which conjoined diaphorically such diverse themes as the visible motion of pushing a ball (since it could be seen rolling a pellet of dung, containing its eggs, along the ground) and the idea of generative potency (since from the invisible eggs new life would mysteriously hatch). Many popular superstitions attached themselves to the dung-beetle too, and the entire mass of such ideas, fused into a general vague notion and attitude, constituted the diaphoric meaning of the symbol for the popular Egyptian consciousness. But the two characteristics I have mentioned played not only a diaphoric but also an archetypal role, since they applied not only to the lowly dung-beetle, but also to the indispensable and lofty sun. The sun bestows a warmth of generative power, and also the sun appears as a ball being rolled across the sky, no doubt by an invisible celestial beetle. The archetypal meaning becomes further reinforced when, in the process of mummification, a gold scarab is substituted for the dead man's heart; for now the meaning of the symbol is extended to include the idea of spiritual regeneration, as the dead man's *ba* (hieroglyphically indicated as a bird) flies upward to be judged by, and then he mystically united with, Osiris.

Or again, take the ancient Egyptian *tau*. Here, too, was a symbol around which many ideas, superstitions, and ritual observations clustered diaphorically. But two of them had such human importance and such associative vitality as to give the symbol an archetypal character. The *tau* was a plug which held back the waters of the rejuvenated Nile and which, when removed, would release them for the irrigation of the land. The *tau* also, by its shape, carried phallic suggestions. Obviously each of these aspects in its own way implies the archetypal idea of new life. Then, when this fused meaning of the *tau* was already several centuries old, a semantic reinforcement was provided by the Christians of Alexandria, who envisaged the *tau* as the Christian Cross with the top prong broken off, and hence as a symbol of spiritually renewed life from yet another standpoint. (The Scandinavian use of the *tau* as an icon of Thor's hammer is extraneous to the development here described, although historically it did introduce certain later complications.)

What bearing has this curious interaction of diaphoric and archetypal modes of activity on myth? One's answer must be particularized, of course, according to the conditions of each specific culture and the nature of the diaphorically combined ideas. Undoubtedly the existence and character of a myth depend upon a variety of conditioning factors, including early man's love of storytelling, his need to explain odd occurrences, his rationalization of ritual, his moral codes, his techniques of magic, and his readiness to retain almost any sufficiently vivid association. I do not underrate the importance of such factors, although they lie outside the boundaries of the present argument. A semantic approach to the matter is not all-sufficient; it may still be very illuminating, however, provided its results are not spoiled by excessive claims of finality. With the same caution and the same limited claim I now proceed to consider the nature of expressive language from the standpoint of its quasi-assertorial elements—i.e., its typical *sentences*.

Naturally, "sentence" is here to be taken functionally rather than grammatically. The single word "snake" (or the equivalent thereof in some primitive language) may function sententially, and in a variety of ways according to the tones in which it is uttered, the gestures that accompany it, and the context (e.g., whether practical or ritualistic) out of which the utterance arises. Any strictly non-sentential unit (e.g., the word "snake" in the logician's or lexicographer's sense) is a later and more sophisticated construct, abstracted from the actual and living occasions on which a snake has been dreaded, pursued, wondered about, worshiped, and the like. Thus the sentence is a vehicle of concrete meaning, whereas the logical terms which can be analytically discovered in it, together with the logical propositions which are built out of them, are vehicles of abstract meaning. Now the language of terms and propositions is the language of logical analysis and of science. The nature of myth is so stubbornly opposed to the nature of these sterner disciplines as to appear, from the empirio-logical standpoint, arbitrary and false. This is the more understandable because myth sometimes irresponsibly borrows elements of literal language and thus appears to be invading the realm of tidy fact more aggressively than was perhaps deliberately intended. Consider, for example, the mythic statement, "God created the world in six days." The awkward intruder here is the final phrase, which brings a false appearance of scientific precision into an affirmation that is properly mythic in the sense of applying the familiar Craftsman idea to a situation that man's natural wonder spontaneously accepts as transcending the understanding. Of course we cannot be sure how the phrase "in six days" was understood by the ancient Jews who presumably originated the mythos, but in any case it tends to blur the nature of the original mythic sentence by giving it the look of a proposition.

Since I wish to explore the possible relationship between primitive sentence-making and myth, I must first ask what is the nature of a sentence in its pre-logical form. Fortunately, we are none of us logical all day long, and we can discover a good deal by noticing how sentences actually function in our more conversational, everyday off-guard moments. This is but a special form of the more general question: What is the semantic role of the non-logical in our familiar discourse? Of course there is more than one way of being non-logical. I am not here speaking of the *il*logical (i.e., a using of logical terms without abiding by the rules they impose) nor of the *sub*logical (as in phatic discourse, the merely perfunctory and vapid), but rather of the expressively *trans*-logical. For in regard to all really important affairs where some degree of valuation and emotional commentary enters, we instinctively recognize the inadequacy of strictly logical forms of speech to do justice to our full intended meanings; and we endeavor by tone of voice, facial expression, and gesture, as well as by choice and arrangement of words, to break through the barriers of prescribed definition and express, no doubt inadequately, the more elusive elements in the situation and in our attitude towards it. Let us call such uses of language "expressive" without any implication that they are therefore to be dismissed as merely subjective and fictional. I am suggesting that in this occasionally spontaneous outreach beyond the the conventional and formal properties of language we are perhaps coming somewhat closer to the conditions of primitive utterance (how close we cannot know) than in our more logical declarations and inquiries. Let us, at any rate, accept the possibility as a working hypothesis, and inquire into the nature of *expressive sentences*.

Since there is a good deal of ambivalence in most human attitudes, it will not be surprising if we find that expressive sentences tend to function in terms of certain polarities. Three such polarities seem to me especially prominent and fundamental. An expressive sentence tends to involve, simultaneously but in varying degree, affirmation and questioning, demanding (or hortation) and acceptance, commitment and stylization. Let us look at these three pairs in turn.

In all the larger affirmations that we make about the world there is likely to be a note of questioning; and this is so because such affirmations touch upon the radical mystery of things, which forever eludes our intellectual grasp. There are two ways of affirming such a sentence as "God created the world." It can be affirmed dogmatically, as a declarative without any interrogative aspect; or it can be affirmed with a fitting intellectual modesty, in which case the declarative and the interrogative will be blended as inseparably as the convex and concave aspects of a single curve. For, to assert it as a pure statement is to imply: "There was a question, but the question is now answered, and thus there is no longer a question." But this can be the case only if the sentence, "God created the world," is essentially intelligible—that is, only if "God," "original creation," and "world" carry meanings that we can put the finger on and say, somewhere in experience, "That is it!" And since this condition—the adequate verification of a transcendental idea by the finite evidences of human experience—cannot possibly be met, it is equally impossible that the sentence, "God created the world," should be a pure statement. To assert it as such is therefore self-delusive. On the other hand there is statement resident in the sentence; a believer does not abandon the declarative element. What he does is to fuse something declarative and something interrogative into a single attitude which is a tension between basic faith and deep questioning. Religiously considered, the sentence employs theological terms symbolically in order to express the radical inseparability of meaningfulness and mystery.

The second polarity which expressive sentences tend to involve—a demanding and an acceptance—brings up the question of wishful thinking. There is likely to be some element of the mandatory—an implicit command, "It shall be so," or an implicit supplication or wish—in all expressive thought and utterance. This is the pragmatic element, which William James found to be present in every judgment, religious and secular, idealistic and materialistic alike, so far as it makes any truth-claim beyond the immediately verifiable connections of direct experience. Inasmuch as religious judgments do make such transcendent truth-claims, the presence of a pragmatic element in them is undeniable. But it is equally important to recognize that the pragmatic element is never the whole affair, and that where it becomes unduly dominant the result is fantasy, not religion. In a truly religious judgment the coercive element, the "Let it be so!," plays a strictly limited role, as an expression of loyalty to a certain general way of conceiving and interpreting the world; in each particular respect it is subordinate to an attitude of acceptance, whatever the grounds and occasions of acceptance may be. The sentence, "God exists," if it represents a mytho-religious affirmation and not simply a metaphysical hypothesis, involves both a demand for a certain way of envisaging the world and an acquiescence towards the obligations which that mode of envisaging entails.

An important contribution to the semantic role of acceptance, or acquiescence, in man's primal form of encounter with the world has been made within the last few decades by those continental thinkers (notably Martin Buber, Franz Rosenzweig, Eugene Rosenstock-Huessy, Karl Löwith, Gabriel Marcel, and Julián Marías) who have stressed the priority of the second grammatical person over the third. The logic of science necessarily employs the third person, because its objects must (linguistically) be spoken *about* and (operationally) be manipulated. It is a widespread assumption, in a world of books and research foundations, that the truth about anything can be adequately revealed (in principle at least) by statements made *about* it. The writers just referred to have challenged this assumption. And there is one sphere of experience where the inadequacy of the *I-it* and the indispensability of the *I-thou* relation is universally recognized —namely in our experience of other human persons. Knowledge of one's fellows, to be more than superficial, must grow out of an experience of mutuality, of speaking to them and listening as they speak in return; and according to all of the above writers, this radical dialectic is what primarily distinguishes the *I-thou* relation from the *I-it*. In more primitive societies it seems probable that, to say the least, the lines between spheres where the *I-thou* relationship could be meaningfully adopted and those where it could not were much less sharply drawn than now. A certain readiness to address nature, or the mysterious presences "behind" nature, and to open one's mind and heart to the "signs of address"[9] which are given in return is a recognizable mark of the primitive attitude.

The third of the sentential polarities—truth-commitments vs. stylization—introduces an idea which I have discussed elsewhere.[10] To start with colloquial instances: when we make a conventional remark about the weather, or when we assure our hostess that we have spent an enjoyable evening, how fully do we commit ourselves to the assertorial content of what we are saying? Not altogether, it is obvious; for in making such remarks we are ordinarily less concerned with the strict truth than with what the immediate situation seems to call for. We recognize them as stylizations, to some degree, in a conversational game, and hence as not committing us to full consistency of belief. Nevertheless, stylization is not quite the whole of it; for while we might phatically applaud the virtues of the weather with a good deal of careless latitude, we would hardly be willing to murmur "Nice day!" (unless with conscious irony) in a downpour of rain. Thus, while the assertorial weight of such conventional remarks (cf. "Having a wonderful time"; *"Mi casa es su casa"; "Vous êtes très gentil"*) stands somewhat above the sheer assertorial zero of the purely exclamatory ("Heigh-ho!"), it does not match the full assertorial weight of an intentionally informative sentence ("It is twenty miles to Woodsville") or a deliberate declaration of value ("That is a dastardly scheme").

The casual instances just cited point the way to analogous but more important instances in the linguistic strategies of poetry, religion, and myth. Coleridge's phrase, "suspension of disbelief," and Richards' doctrine of the "pseudo-statement" represent attempts of both critics to explain how it is that although the sentences employed in poetry seem to be making statements of a kind, they often cannot be accepted with anything like full commitment of assent. But as I have argued elsewhere,[11] I believe that Richards errs by making too sharp a dichotomy between "statements" (claimants for exact verification by scientific method) and "pseudo-statements" (word-patterns which look like statements and which serve to organize certain emotive attitudes in the prepared reader, but to which any question of truth or falsity is entirely irrelevant). The most interesting examples of poetic statement fall somewhere between these extremes: they invite some degree of assent, but less than full intellectual commitment.

As we turn from primarily poetic sentences to primarily religious sentences (admitting, of course, a wide area of overlapping) we find that the relation between commitment and stylization is characteristically somewhat different. A genuinely religious believer is one who gives full commitment—not necessarily to the sentences in their literal meanings and in any case not in their literal meanings alone, but to some half-guessed, half-hidden truth which the sentences symbolize. (Let it not be forgotten that the early Fathers of the Church were wont to speak of their articles of faith, in which they certainly "believed," as *symbola*.) The commitment in such a case does not necessarily diminish as the stylization of liturgy and figurative language is increased (although extreme Protestants have sometimes made the mistake of supposing that it must do so); for the commitment may be given in and through the stylized forms. In short there may be full commitment here, but it is largely commitment by indirection. I say "largely," not "wholly," because a typically religious believer is likely to feel some degree of commitment to the concrete vehicle (e.g., the Virgin Birth, the avatars of Vishnu, the magical connection between pipe smoke and thunder clouds, etc.) as well as to the transcendental tenor (the real but hardly sayable significance of these doctrines for the serious believer). The literal meaning of the vehicle is usually clear and vivid, although perhaps shocking to everyday standards of probability; its transcendental tenor looms darkly behind the scene as something vague, inarticulate, yet firmly intuited and somehow of tremendous, even final, importance and consequentiality. To accept the vehicle in its literal aspect exclusively is the way of superstition; to accept its transcendental references (the tenor) exclusively is the way of allegory. The primitively mytho-religious attitude in its most characteristic forms has tended to settle into some kind of fertile tension between these two extremes without yielding too completely to either of them. So far as the mythic storyteller is half-consciously aware of the tension his narrative may achieve that tone of serious playfulness which characterizes so charmingly much early myth.

The hypothesis with which I now conclude connects the earlier and later parts of my paper, and is offered tentatively, as suggesting certain possibilities of further research. Perhaps the line between the primary and romantic phases of myth, although vague and wavering at best, can be drawn a little more clearly by the aid of such semantic criteria as I have been discussing. Primitive myths may be regarded as the early expressions of man's storytelling urge so far as it is still conditioned by such proto-linguistic tendencies as diaphoric ambiguity and the several kinds of sentential polarity. Later myths, and later retellings of the earlier myths, betray their essentially romantic character by the degree to which such semantic fluidity and plenitude have been exchanged for tidier narratives relying on firmer grammatical, logical, and causal relationships. In its propaedeutic aspect the hypothesis invites a more active liaison between semantics, broadly conceived, and anthropology—a collaboration which might prove to have fruitful consequences for both disciplines.

NOTES

1. Alan W. Watts, *Myth and Ritual in Christianity* (London, 1953), p. 7.

2. Ernst Cassirer, *Die Philosophie der symbolischen Formen,* Vol. II: *Mythisches Denken* (Berlin, 1923-1929).

3. Lucien Lévy-Bruhl, *How Natives Think* (London, 1926), chap. 2. Susanne Langer, *Philosophy in a New Key* (Cambridge, Mass., 1942), chap. 7.

4. Richard Chase, *Quest for Myth* (Baton Rouge, 1949), p. 73; cf. p. 110, et passim.

5. Philip Wheelwright, *The Burning Fountain: A Study in the Language of Symbolism* (Bloomington, Ind., 1954), chaps. 2, 4, et passim.

6. Herbert Read, *English Prose Style,* rev. ed. (New York, 1952).

7. Aristotle, *Poetics,* chap. 21.

8. Chief Standing Bear, *Land of the Spotted Eagle* (Boston, 1933), p. 201. Cf. Hartley Burr Alexander, *The World's Rim: Great Mysteries of the North American Indians* (Lincoln, Neb., 1953), chap. 1, "The Pipe of Peace," where the above passage is also quoted.

9. The phrase is Martin Buber's. See his *Between Man and Man* (London, 1947), especially Part I, "Dialogue."

10. Wheelwright, *The Burning Fountain,* pp. 66-70, 274-282.

11. Wheelwright, *The Burning Fountain,* pp. 33-36, 45-50, 296-298.

MYTH AND FOLKTALES

BY STITH THOMPSON

W HEN I agreed many months ago to add to this symposium some remarks about the relation of myth and
folktale, the editor suggested that I might wish to comment
on the other papers which form a part of this series, and he
very kindly placed them at my disposal in manuscript.[1] I
shall, however, confine myself largely to my own subject
and only incidentally refer to the other papers.

As I have taken time out to prepare this paper, I find myself in the midst of the revision of my *Motif-Index of Folk-
Literature* where for many months, and, indeed, many years
I have been in daily contact with thousands of narrative
motifs from all parts of the world. These motifs, of course,
have come from many places, but they all belong to the large
area of traditional literature. An exercise of this kind has a
tendency to keep one's feet definitely on the ground and to
discourage theorizing. One is daily impressed with the variety of cultural patterns in all parts of the world and becomes
suspicious of general statements about them. Generalizations
made for Central Polynesia will probably have very little in
common with those made for the marginal peoples of South

America, or the Congo tribes of Central Africa. Insofar as all
these people are human and have human needs, there will be
similar acts and thoughts because of the limitation of possibilities in solving human problems. The origins of myths and
folktales over the world must be extremely diverse, so that
it is not safe to posit any single origin even for those of a
particular people.

Such is the general attitude to which this purely empirical
approach has led me. To many this will seem only a negative
reaction for I have no answer to make to those who claim to
know exactly where myths came from and how they are
related to tales.

In spite of this bias against what seems to me oversimplifi-
cation, I have taken time to reread a good deal of literature
upon mythology and to discuss it in some detail with a very
excellent seminar of graduate students at Indiana University. This quest began with the general question of what
people were talking about when they discussed myth; but
most of the authors who have written about myth make very
little effort to connect their work with such myths as one
actually finds when he reads collections from all parts of the
world. We need not now consider the recent perversions of
the word "myth" which some of the modern literary critics
are employing. Most of the writers whom we read in this
seminar do at least refer, generally speaking, to stories that
have become traditional. But of those traditional stories,
which ones shall be called myth, which ones legends and
traditions (the German *Sagen*), which shall be called folktales, and which animal tales—all of that never seems very
clear to the reader of many books on mythology. Among the
writers of the present symposium, there seems, however, to
be some agreement. All agree that stories about the gods and
their activities in general are myths. But shall we also include hero tales? I imagine that Raglan and Hyman would.
Wheelwright would include them perhaps under his second
stage. I doubt whether any of the others would speak of his
third category of myth, that which he calls the consummatory, at all. It would seem to me only to add great confusion
to an already confused subject.

When reviewing the treatments of myth sometimes as originally presented and sometimes in excellent summaries —such as those of Bidney where one passes from Euhemerus and the ancients through the mediaeval allegorizors, through the Brothers Grimm and the weather-myth advocates; and the sun-myth, astral-myth, and moon-myth schools which Dorson had so well reviewed for us; through Freud and Jung and Erich Fromm, Roheim, Saintyves, and Malinowski, and some at least of the imposing array of writers on the ritualistic theory—one continually gets a sense of unreality, of living in a world of phantasmagoria, in a never-never land where nothing every says what it means, or means what it says, where people have only one thought and only one interest. They are either contemplating day in and day out the movements of the sun and are never able to tell a simple story without dragging the sun in, as Mr. Dick always had to drag in the execution of Charles I. Or they may be a world of stargazers, who, instead of looking around them and telling tales of the men and beasts with which they are acquainted, must always tell stories about the stars, or if not actually about the stars, stories which meant the stars to their ancestors. But then we find that that is all a mistaken impression, that the moon is the center of attention of all peoples, especially primitive peoples, and in spite of manifest evidence to the contrary, that all stories and myths are made up of the moon and its phases and its monthly course, its eclipses and its effects upon terrestrial life. But all these ideas are negated when it is realized that the actual reason for the existence of stories about the gods, and perhaps about the heroes, is the fact that there are certain psychological compulsions which impel people to tell tales of particular kinds. Dreams, fears, and stresses—it is from these that come the gods, the heroes, and the tales about them. Whether these patterns are thought of in the terms of Freud or Jung or Erich Fromm does not matter much. If Jung is right, Freud is wrong. If Fromm is right, Jung and Freud are wrong. Unless, therefore, the searcher is very persistent, he is likely to look elsewhere for the explanation of his myths, especially after he reads some of the fantastic explanations given to stories which he knows very well. By this time he is prepared to pass into a *selva oscura* even more revolting and unlikely, a world filled with phallic symbols and fertility rites.

At journey's end, we come to the ritual origin and we observe something that no anthropologist has told us about— that all the rituals in the world have a single pattern and a single purpose, and that the only way a story could be made up originally was in imitation of a ritual. But though they show some undoubted instances of this occurrence, none of these writers tells us how the ritual itself evolved and how the inventive process which moved from ritual into a story about the gods and heroes is any easier than any other form of invention.

All the writers we have mentioned, as well as the philosophers such as those Bidney discusses, approach the problem of the origin of myth as if it were capable of a single solution. It is this monistic approach that brings each of them to claim finality and to say categorically that all others are wrong. If one is devoted to a particular faith, he must have no traffic with heretics.

After this experience with the writers on mythology of the last century or more, one comes back to safer ground and resumes his quest for a definition that will afford a central point of attack. But why should myth be accurately defined? Is there actually any need to differentiate, for example, between such concepts as mythology and hero tales? It would seem that the only possible use of definitions of this kind is to enable us to name something when we see it. This means that a useful definition of myth must be substantive, it must declare that certain kinds of material form the subject of myth and certain kinds do not. I find myself astonished that Raglan should begin his article by saying that a myth is simply a narrative associated with a rite. He then proceeds to show that a myth (that is, a narrative associated with a rite) is indeed associated with a rite. I feel certain that he did not mean to make such a circular statement as this serve as a definition, for later in the paper it turns out that not only myths, but ballads, folktales and *Sagen* are also associated with rites and, that therefore this special association breaks down as a definition. The other supporter of the ritual theory,

Hyman, apparently hopes to include practically all human activities—dance and jazz and we know not what else—so that eventually from a single ritualistic act of a single type of ritual all of narrative art can eventually be traced. The ritualistic school seems little concerned with the definition of myth.

And yet there is a practical value in defining myths according to the type of subject matter they include and not according to their origin, since their origin is one of the very points at issue. The practical definition which I have suggested and which seems to be rather well agreed upon is that myth has to do with the gods and their actions, with creation, and with the general nature of the universe and of the earth. This is a minimum definition, for it must be recognized that the word myth is frequently used with a much broader meaning. If we confine ourselves to European literature, we find myth sometimes applied also to the hero tales, whether those hero tales deal with demigods or not. Ovid, in his *Metamorphoses,* seems to have considered that he was dealing with myths, and here his criterion was that of primordial transformation. He must also have considered one purpose of myth to be the explanation of some existing forms in nature. But as in so many so-called etiological myths, the explanation which he gives is nearly always merely tacked on and is certainly not the reason for the existence of the tale. This often happens with stories of primitive peoples: explanations are added almost as an afterthought to an ordinary folktale. In the past too much weight has certainly been given to the importance of the explanatory elements in myths. It is frequently there, as any one who reads the literature can testify, but it is not important enough to constitute an actual definition of myth.

As we get away from Western cultures and enter the circle of more primitive peoples, there is less concern about separation of folktales into the mythical and non-mythical. This fact is vividly brought out in any bibliography of North American Indian tales. The authors of such collections call them with seeming indifference tales, myths, legends, or traditions. Some students of these primitive tales have indeed observed that the tribes themselves have a tendency to differentiate between ordinary tales and those about an ancient world preceding the present. But in this respect there is the greatest difference between individual tribes, and a strict classification of these tales into myths and non-myths is quite impossible.

Another aspect of the myths of primitive peoples which makes any such differentiation difficult is the way in which their superior beings, whether thought of actually as gods or as culture heroes, are usually treated in two aspects, one of them serious and the other in which the god or hero is the center of buffoonery. Wherever this trickster-hero idea occurs there is a tendency to tell of the foolish trickster at any time, but to confine the tales of the serious culture hero to special occasions, sometimes at rituals and sometimes merely at the proper hour or proper season.

With such a group as the North American Indians, then, it is often possible to speak of certain tales as essentially mythological because they deal with origins and with higher powers. But in the study of a particular tale, as it spreads over the continent, it is often impossible to know whether the native teller thinks of it as myth or ordinary story. Mostly the question never occurs to him. For, in spite of the distinction that has just been drawn, it refers to only a very small group of the hero tales, and for most of the rest of the body of folk narrative for primitive peoples everywhere, any differentiation between ordinary tale and myth is very minor.

Whether we use the strict definition of myth suggested or include hero tales and those of animal origins, there is a point at which any confusion between folktale and myth ceases. The European fairy tales, for example "Cinderella" and "Snow White," have few of the usual characteristics of myth. They are filled, of course, with the supernatural, but most narratives going back a long way *are* filled with the supernatural. In Europe, at least, they generally function as pure fiction and are not the subjects of real belief. Yet there is a difficulty in any such assertion, because stories with exactly the same plots are frequently told among tribes where they seem to be implicitly believed in. The attempts to define *Märchen* or fairy tale turn out to be almost as unsatisfactory as those to make a strict definition of myth. The two forms continually flow into each other, and it is likely that the dis-

tinction between *Märchen* and other types of folk narrative
is largely confined to Western culture. Though some corre-
spondences exist in other continents, it would be a mistake
to try to carry over to the rest of the world the definitions
made on the basis of European collections.

Since these *genre* are not really valid applied to a world-
wide study of folk narrative, it must be recognized that when
we use such European terms as myth, etiological story,
Märchen, Sage, or the like, we are merely using these terms
as points of reference and we must understand that they have
only vague analogues in various countries of the world. The
primitive tale-teller cares little for such distinctions. Even
in the European setting, the scholar finds that for most kinds
of problems such differentiation is of small importance.

Even if we were able to reach more satisfactory definitions
we would only have made ready for other objects of study in
the field of myth and folktale. Nearly all of the writers cited
in this paper manifest great interest in origins. Where did
myth and folktales come from? How were they invented in
the first place? We have earlier suggested some of the answers given to this intriguing question. The greatest difficulty with writers on the subject in the past has been their
slowness to recognize that the problem is not simple. We are
dealing with some thousands of tales, many hundreds of them
certainly mythological. These occur in all parts of the world
and in tribes of the most diverse cultures. It must be recognized that each myth and each tale constitutes a problem in
itself if one is to know its life history. One can, of course, take
high ground, as many of the schools already mentioned have
done, and tell us offhand that all myths and all tales have
come to us by a particular favored route. The problem, however, is surely not "where do myths come from?" but rather
"where does each individual myth come from?" Every myth
has its own history as every folktale has its own history. Even
the adherents of some of the monistic schools already mentioned recognize the vast amount of give and take there has
always been in the behavior of myths and folktales. But while
they give lip service to dissemination, they seldom give sufficient weight to the facts of cultural borrowing.

It is always easier to borrow a myth or a tale than it is to construct one. The body of narratives of any particular primitive people is not likely to exceed several hundred, and of these several hundred it is usually possible to find that the great majority are held in common with their neighbors. Now such simple facts as this must be thoroughly worked out and understood before one begins to talk about the origins of a story. From this point of view there is no distinction whatever between the ordinary folktale and the myth. They both disseminate, they both take on accretions and are subject to the vicissitudes of memory and forgetting. Before any search for origins is proper, one should ideally know all the facts of the history of the item which is being studied. Of course not all of the facts can be known, but there is a scholarly obligation to know as many of them as possible. If a scholar is going to work with a folktale, for example, he must have before him all the known versions, even though these may run to a thousand. If he analyses these and takes into consideration all of the historic facts available and studies his geography well, he may be able to see something of the general place of origin and of the vague earliest form of the story he is studying. And he may be able to explain much of the subsequent history of the tale.

Can he go back to the actual origin? I am in great doubt whether he can go further than to trace the full-blooded tale or myth to its earliest known home. If one is a folktale student, one can, of course, speculate as to the way in which various motifs have been brought together to constitute a certain tale. But though I have concerned myself for half a lifetime with the history of narrative motifs, I am very skeptical of any success in working out what we may call the prehistory of a particular tale or myth. Naturally, the fact that I am skeptical about this does not mean that it cannot be done. Perhaps when we know enough about all the various myths and tales and have studied them carefully and objectively through proper analysis, we may be able to come to some general conclusions about particular classes of them. But the ultimate origin of nearly all folktales and myths must remain a mystery, just as the origin of language is a mystery. There is of course nothing mystical about it: it is merely impossible to recapture the needed facts. And in the absence of the facts, I would wish to leave the ultimate origin of any tale or myth with a large question mark rather than with a dubious answer. I prefer the methods of the student now writing a dissertation on one of the best known of all folktales. He has laboriously assembled about a thousand versions from all parts of the world and has studied them analytically. Though he cannot tell us exactly where and when and why this tale was first told, he had as nearly as possible all the facts available, and he will certainly be wary of accepting easy answers.

With such a background he will certainly not take the interpretations of Saintyves seriously. So far as I know, no living folktale specialist today does so, for Saintyves was obviously not concerned with the life history of the tales he discussed. The story which is cited in Raglan's paper exists in not fewer than a thousand known versions, none of which would indicate any connection with the French ritual he is talking about.

A coordinate question to that just discussed is often heard in connection with myths and tales; that is, what do they mean? Frequently this is asked as a general question, and as such has no meaning to me. But often the matter is put much more specifically, so that we ask, "What does the tale of Cupid and Psyche mean?" I am inclined to agree with Bidney and to say that it means what it says. One important function of tales has been to fulfill pleasantly man's leisure, and there seems to be no evidence from those who have been familiar with storytellers in all parts of the world to make us believe that men everywhere cannot invent persons and scenes and project them upon a background, natural or supernatural, so as to make a story. It seems incredible that the further we go back, the more philosophical the tales should become, that they should contain allegories, or that the characters should represent heavenly bodies or stages of the weather. The psychoanalytical interpretations of various stories and myths seems equally unlikely, but they cannot all be dismissed lightly. Each one has to be studied on its own merits. It happens that those I have seen discussed in the books of various psychoanalysts have been handled quite fantastically. But this should not blind one to the fact that perhaps some of these interpretations have value. On the whole, however, a quest for meanings outside the tale or myth itself is doomed to failure, because we simply do not know the frame of mind of the unknown person in the unknown place and the unknown time and the unknown culture who first contrived the story. The search for the original meaning of any folk story is quite as impossible as the search for the origin of that story. For both quests adequate data are missing. We are left with a choice of making a guess according to our own predilections or of saying that we do not know. It is by all means preferable to say that we do not know.

It has just been suggested that one of the reasons for the invention of tales and myths is the filling in of leisure time. It is not only in modern Western culture that relief from boredom has been sought, though elsewhere this is often masked as something that seems more worthy—religious ceremonial, magic dance, a tale for the edification of youth, a pious commemorative exercise in honor of saint or ancestor. Actually such motives are very much mixed, but the man who can fill pleasantly with story or anecdote the long watches of the night or the tedious days of voyage or caravan must always have been a treasured companion, and the breaking up of the daily routine by ceremonies and saint's day holidays, not to speak of camp meetings and religious revivals in Protestant countries—these activities are far from being exclusively religious. Tales and myths do, of course, have their practical uses aside from mere amusement or pastime. It is this great variety of function that has given rise to so many theories of their origin and meaning. Investigators of one group of people see one aspect of the narrative and its function, and are likely to report such as the exclusive purpose of these human activities. No three blind men ever investigated the essential nature of the elephant with more surprising results than those who have sought the single answer which would unlock the mystery of the origin and nature of tales and myths.

Yet, for some parts of the world and for some special conditions, it is likely that hardly one of the upholders of theories which we have noticed has been altogether wrong. It would doubtless be rewarding for those who reject these single solutions of the origin of myth and tale to reread the works of the proponents of these theories and see whether or not at least a few of the examples they cite may be valid. Part of the elephant after all was actually like a rope. If one is examining the myths and folktales of a group of South American Indians, he will find that he is moving in a considerably different world from that which he encounters in stories of the Indians of the North Pacific Coast or the natives of Polynesia. There have doubtless been actual sun-myths and star-myths and moon-myths, and I am persuaded by reading in Laistner and in von der Leyen's book on the folktale that some myths and tales may have come from dreams—always, of course, in terms of life as known by the dreamer. Though I find myself extremely resistant to the suggestion, I know that certain of my friends, well acquainted at firsthand with the stories of certain primitive peoples, are persuaded that occasionally psychoanalytical interpretations of some variety do actually apply. And my objection to the ritualistic school is not based upon a disbelief in the possibility of ritual producing myth or to doubt as to its actual occurrence in the Mediterranean area and sometimes in unlettered tribes of Australia and North America. It is to the exclusive claims of all these schools that objection is to be raised.

Finally, it should be pointed out that after a century or more of discussion we seem to know almost as little as ever about the mutual relations of the various types of oral narrative. That sometimes one form does lead into another cannot be denied, but this is likely to be a local manifestation and not something operating as a world-wide evolution. Only purely theoretical considerations would suggest an inevitable order, such as Raglan does in his book on *The Hero:* ritual—drama—ballad—tale. Students of the folk literature of the North American Indians will find such a suggestion fantastic. It happens that my own initiation into folktale studies came from this very quest. In those days, a half-century ago, there was a general feeling that the balad preceded prose as a form of folk narrative. When I wished to investigate this matter among the North American Indians, a wise professor told me to get hold of a dozen American Indian stories told in poetic form. I searched the literature for weeks and found none, and except for a few extremely simple narrative chants, fifty years of rather close observation has failed to bring any such narrative poems to light. And yet, among these same peoples, not one tribe fails to have a good collection of myths and folktales.

The problems presented by myths and tales will certainly not be finally solved by this generation. We may be sure that a century from now students will still be analyzing and trying to reach some kind of syntheses of their analytical results, and by that time there may be a sufficient corps of scholars to investigate form and style as manifested in folk narrative. By that time we may well have settled the question as to whether there ever was a myth-making age, or whether we shall have to agree that the forces making for myths and tales are still active wherever conditions are right. Other monistic theories will doubtless be advanced and all of us will seem extremely old-fashioned; but it would be interesting to look at all these matters through their eyes and to see how our theories and ideas appear after a hundred years.

NOTE

1. The author had no opportunity to read the manuscripts of Lévi-Strauss and Eggan. [Ed.]

A selected list of MIDLAND BOOKS

MB-1	OVID'S METAMORPHOSES *translated by Rolfe Humphries* (cloth $4.95)	$1.95
MB-2	OVID'S THE ART OF LOVE *translated by Rolfe Humphries*	$1.85
MB-3	THE LOVE ETHIC OF D. H. LAWRENCE *by Mark Spilka*	$1.75
MB-4	SANTAYANA AND THE SENSE OF BEAUTY *by Willard Arnett*	$1.85
MB-6	THE DIPLOMACY OF THE AMERICAN REVOLUTION *by Samuel Flagg Bemis*	$1.95
MB-7	THE LITERARY SYMBOL *by William York Tindall*	$1.95
MB-8	GEOFFREY CHAUCER *by John Livingston Lowes*	$1.95
MB-12	THE DOUBLE *by F. M. Dostoyevsky, tr. George Bird*	$1.75
MB-13	PAUL GAUGUIN'S INTIMATE JOURNALS *translated and edited by Van Wyck Brooks* (52 illustrations) (cloth $3.95)	$1.95
MB-14	AFRICAN NOTEBOOK *by Albert Schweitzer* (illus.) (cloth $3.95)	$1.75
MB-15	THE MORAL DECISION *by Edmond Cahn* (cloth $5.00)	$2.25
MB-16	FORMS OF MODERN FICTION *edited by William Van O'Connor*	$1.75
MB-19	THE ESTHETIC BASIS OF GREEK ART *by Rhys Carpenter* (illustrated)	$1.75
MB-20	THE SATIRES OF JUVENAL *translated by Rolfe Humphries* (cloth $3.75)	$1.65
MB-21	FREEDOM AND CIVILIZATION *by Bronislaw Malinowski*	$2.25
MB-22	JOHN DRYDEN: A STUDY OF HIS POETRY *by Mark Van Doren*	$1.75
MB-23	THE MANAGERIAL REVOLUTION *by James Burnham*	$1.95
MB-24	AGE OF SURREALISM *by Wallace Fowlie* (illustrated)	$1.75
MB-25	COLERIDGE ON IMAGINATION *by I. A. Richards*	$1.95
MB-26	JAMES JOYCE AND THE MAKING OF ULYSSES *by Frank Budgen*	$2.25
MB-27	THE LIFE OF SCIENCE *by George Sarton, introduction by Conway Zirkle*	$1.50
MB-29	THE THREE WORLDS OF ALBERT SCHWEITZER *by Robert Payne*	$1.75
MB-30	OXFORD LECTURES ON POETRY *by A. C. Bradley*	$2.45
MB-31	ASPECTS OF FORM *edited by Lancelot Law Whyte* (illus.)	$1.95
MB-32	ART AND INDUSTRY *by Herbert Read* (138 illustrations)	$1.95
MB-33	THE TALES OF RABBI NACHMAN *by Martin Buber, translated by Maurice Friedman*	$1.95
MB-34	MAGIC AND SCHIZOPHRENIA *by Géza Róheim* (cloth $5.00)	$2.25
MB-35	THE HISTORY OF SCIENCE AND THE NEW HUMANISM *by George Sarton*	$1.95
MB-36	THE GOLDEN ASS *by Apuleius, translated by Jack Lindsay*	$1.85
MB-37	MUSIC IN AMERICAN LIFE *by Jacques Barzun*	$1.75
MB-38	DANTE'S LA VITA NUOVA *translated by Mark Musa*	$1.65
MB-40	THE DISCOVERY OF LANGUAGE: LINGUISTIC SCIENCE IN THE NINETEENTH CENTURY *by Holger Pedersen, tr. by John Webster Spargo* (illustrated) (cloth $6.50)	$2.95
MB-41	THE PARADOX OF TRAGEDY *by D. D. Raphael* (cloth $3.00)	$1.45
MB-42	AN INTRODUCTION TO THE GREEK THEATRE *by Peter D. Arnott*	$2.45
MB-43	REFLECTIONS ON THE DEATH OF A PORCUPINE *by D. H. Lawrence*	$1.95
MB-45	VERGIL'S AENEID *translated, with an introduction and notes by L. R. Lind* (cloth $5.75)	$1.95
MB-46	ESSAYS ON THE ODYSSEY: SELECTED MODERN CRITICISM *edited by Charles H. Taylor, Jr.* (cloth $6.00)	$1.95
MB-47	THE LIVING THOUGHTS OF KIERKEGAARD *presented by W. H. Auden*	$1.95
MB-48	THE QUESTION OF JEAN-JACQUES ROUSSEAU *by Ernst Cassirer, translated and edited by Peter Gay*	$1.65
MB-49	THE NEW APOLOGISTS FOR POETRY *by Murray Krieger*	$2.25

(continued on next page)

PB 30025-SB